Indian English Literature and Popular Culture : An Overview

Indian English Literature and Popular Culture

An Overview

Dr. Sachinkumar R. Pandya

PACIFIC BOOKS INTERNATIONAL

Indian English Literature and Popular Culture : An Overview

First Published : 2017

ISBN 978-93-86655-57-8

Published by :
PACIFIC BOOKS INTERNATIONAL
108, 1st Floor, 4832/24, Prahlad Street,
Ansari Road, Daryaganj, New Delhi - 110002
Phone : 011-23268444, Mob. : 09212526400
e-mail : pacificbooks@rediffmail.com,
pacificbooksinternational@gmail.com

Laser Typesetting by :
Vedansh Computers
Delhi - 110009

Printed at :
Roshan Offset Printers
Delhi

Preface

The book has been written to meet the requirements of scholars in the field of Indian Writing in English. The purpose of this book is twofold: it zooms in onto a topic from a multi dimensional approach – a critical analysis and revealing many aspects of the issues in Indian English Literature. The other is it can easily zoom the cultural issue that is prevailing nowadays.

The specifically designed eye-view is to ensure the scholars, students any assistance and to focus the general approach to Indian English Literature and Popular Culture.

Henceforth, the book carries a certain amount of creativity on the side of elite class to progress on their own as well.

At this juncture, I thank my parents, my family members, my gurus, my colleagues and friends to help me whenever I needed.

I especially thank Lord Saibaba and my dear son, Tathya who inspired me a lot.

Dr. Sachinkumar R. Pandya

Contents

1

Introduction

The Indian English Novel comprises of the various phases of changes in its history and the history of the nation. It has grown and developed throughout its history by contributions from Indian Languages in translation and by the use of English language to the authentic means for expressing one's ideas, thoughts, concepts and imagination. Earlier, the education was not in growth and speaking English was inessential. It has attained maturity, but it is not that it fatly emerged from nowhere. It has had its phases of development. The stories were already there- in the legends, in the folklore and the local languages and cultures that gossiped, conversed, laughed and cried all over India. India has been a land of Kathas always, the delineation between ritual and reality was very subtle. Indian writers have made the most significant contribution to the field of the novel writing in English. From the publication of Bankim Chandra Chatterjee's *Rajmohan's Wife* in the year 1864, Indian novel has grown significantly in bulkiness, variety and got maturity. What began as a small plant has now attained a luxuriant tree and outspreaded in various directions. The progress of Indian novel follows certain specific patterns, and it is not difficult to mark out its gradual development from the imitative stage to the realistic to psychological to the experimental stage. The Indian novels in English erupted in the fiery talks of Henry Derozio, the spiritual prose of Tagore and the pacifist dictums given by Gandhi. With the coming of Mulk Raj Anand, Raja Rao and R.K. Narayan, the Indian English novels had begun its voyage.

A great crop of Indian writing English and its prominence achieved by winning many literary medals towards the end of the 20th is indicative of the widespread national and international identification it has achieved over the period of time. The Indian English Novel, moreover, has now been widely much-admired all over the world, as it has been successful in shaping its own position not only in the world of commonwealth literature but also in the 'World literature'. Though the origin of Indian literature in English as a whole is necessarily the English education and the preface to British literature, the Indian English Novel came forward as a necessary product of its own story telling tradition and the tradition of English novel. So, it is considered that one of the most worth mentioning gifts of English education to India is prose fiction for though India was probably a top fountain of story-telling, the novel as we know today was an importation from the West.

Popular literature includes those writings planned for the masses and those that find favors with bulky audiences. It can be different from artistic literature in the sense that it is designed mainly to entertain. Unlike high literature, popular literature generally doesn't seek a high degree of formal beauty or delicacy and is not proposed to endure. The development of popular literature has paralleled the spread of literacy through education and has been facilitated by scientific developments in printing. With the Industrial Revolution, works of literature, which were previously produced for using up by small, learned elites, became available to large sections and even the most of the members of a population. The border line between artistic and popular literature is misty, with much traffic between the two categories as current public preference and later critical assessment. While he was alive Shakespeare could be thought of as an author of popular literature, but now, he is regarded as a creator of artistic literature. Certainly, the main method of defining a work as belonging to popular literature is whether it is ephemeral,that is, losing its demand and importance with the passage of time. The most significant genre in popular literature is and forever has been the romance, extending as it does from the medieval ages to the present. The most common type of romance describes the obstacles encountered by two people -usually young-busy in a forbidden love. Another common genre is that of fantasy, or science fiction. Novels set in the western frontier of the U. S. in the nineteenth century, and called westerns, are also popular. Finally, the detective story or murder mystery is a broadly read kind of popular literature. Popular literature has also come to contain such genres as comic books and cartoon strips. There were the days when Indian writing in English was termed derivative and initiative: it has achieved free identity today. From Tagore to Naipaul, Indian English has gained international recognition.

The record of Indian Literature in English can be very much aliened to the arrival and supreme reign of the British upon India. The kingdom did have its both merits and demerits. Leaving out brutal colonization, Britishers did leave their astonishing qualities in the field of architectural, political and literary sides. It was also specifically during time that Indian Literatures, in an envious attempt to show their revolt against English works of art, came out on the globe.

Indian Writing In English: Overview

The truth that Indian literatures are a product of a multilingual, multicultural and socio-historical mixture cannot be ignored. Nowadays, Indian literature reached at the zenith of creation with the involvement of regional and national writers. The researcher would like to focus on the origin and brief literary history of Indian English literature and the genre – novel in Indo-Anglian literature up to the time of Mulk Raj Anand. At this point, it is necessary to state the brief history of Indian writing in English and its contributors. Besides the list of the contributors in Indian writing in English, the rise of the new form of literature-novel writing in India is also essential to focus. For that one would like to divide the history of Indian writing in English into three parts. First, to recognize the commencement and exploration of Indian English literature by key contributors, second, for the rise and growth of new literary form (novel) in Indian literature and third, to understand Mulkraj Anand as a novelist. Indo-Anglian literature contributed to the common pool of world writing in English. It is a literature which is a amalgamation of Indian literature and Indian literature written in English language. Indian Literature in English refers to the body of work by Indian writers who write in English and whose native or co-native language could be one of the several languages of India. It is also connected with the works of the writers of the Indian Diaspora. It is often referred to as Indo- Anglian literature. As a category, this production comes under the broader territory of postcolonial literature- the production from formerly colonized countries like India. Indian literature in English has a pretty recent history; it is only one and a half centuries old.

The first book written in English by an Indian was by Sake Dean Mahomet, titled *Travels of Dean Mahomet*; Mahomet's travelling tale was published in 1793 in England. In its beginning stages, it was influenced by the Western art form of the novel. Early Indian writers used English untouched by Indian words to express an experience which was essentially Indian. Indian English literature is a product of the historical encounter amid the two cultures—Indian and the western—for about one hundred and ninety years. It isn't that Indian inhabitants didn't experience the impact of a foreign culture. It did during the reigns of various foreign rulers. But the variation with the British rule lies in the nature of the financial system that had come into being in Europe after the Renaissance as depicted by Marx as capitalist system. Before the beginning of the British rule, India had the feudal economic scheme, in accordance with which the much population of the country, who have various religious faiths and conforming to the caste system, tried to live their life, fatalistically and sometimes stoically sometimes. Above all, it was a closed society with a strange cultural racial prejudice. In fact, India had been awaiting cultural and political change, which became essential after the fading and collapse of the Mogul Empire. First of all, British rule in India, resulted in breaking the obstacle of that closed society. Then the greatest cultural effect came with the establishment of four universities and with the beginning of western educational system. The British language provided the natives with a way to the western literature and to the western culture, of course. This type of education created a class of native bourgeoisie, the majority of which turned to their native language while giving birth to a native literature, applying the western aesthetic norms. But a few amongst them thought it proper to give expressions to their feelings and experiences in English. Thus, the peculiar body of Indian English literature was created—while its contents were to be Indian, its means of expression was English.

If we take a backward look at the beginnings of Indo-Anglian literature, the strong figure of Raja Rammohan Roy seems first. The renaissance begins with Raja Rammohan Roy in modern Indian literature. He had earned good control over English language by working with British officials. He had tried to give new eye view, removed old belief and typical rituals through Bramhosamaj. The Bramhosamaj encourages establishing tuning between men's traditional faith and their practical observations. Rammohan Roy worked for the betterment of women, freedom of in the field of journalism, English education, social justice and dilemma of Indian peasantry. He had good command English and wrote prose and poetry in it. K.R.

Srinivasa Iyengar believes that Rammohan Roy although he could be named as the first of the Indian masters of English prose, was great in so fields that be belong to Indian history more than to simple Indo-Anglian literary history. In this way, he had contributed his writing and thoughts in the groundwork of Indo-Anglian literature and prepared way for his successors and colleagues like Henry Derozio, the Cavally Brothers, Kashiproshad Ghose, Hasan Ali, P. Rajagopual, Mohanlal, and Michel Madhusudan Dutt etc., are considered first Indo-Anglian writers of poetry and prose.

The mid 19th century is the renaissance in India as that was the time of great literary and social upheavals. At that time legendary writers like Maharshi Debendranath Tagore, Kesub Chunder Sen, Dayanand Saraswati, the founder of the Arya Samaj have contributed for social transformation, educational modification and religious reform which has given scope for renaissance in India. The first English poet in India, Henry Louis Vivian Derozio (1809-1831) had nurtured English poetry in India. He became a lecturer of English literature at the Hindu College, Kolkata. A teacher and a poet, Derozio had expressed nature in his poetry like Keats. The taste of Romanticism found in his poetry as he was highly influenced by Byron, Shelley, Keats, Scott and Moore. He died at the very early age due to cholera. This was the time when Hindu civilization in Bengal was undergoing considerable uproar. In 1828, Raja Ram Mohan Roy established the Brahmo Samaj, which kept Hindu ideals but denied idolization. This resulted in a criticism within traditional Hindu society. Even though Derozio himself was an atheist and had left Christianity, he encouraged questioning the orthodox Hindu traditions and conventions on the basis of Judeo-Christian rationalism. He fused in his students the spirit of free expression, the thirst for knowledge and a passion to live up to their individuality, while inquiring illogical religious and cultural practices. Derozio's intense enthusiasm for teaching and his communications with students created a sensation at Hindu College. His students came to be known as Derozians. He organized debates where ideas and social norms were freely debated. Iyengar took great delight in his exchanges with students, writing about them:

> Expanding like the petals of young flowers I watch the gentle opening of your minds.[1] *(Iyengar : 1995,33)*

Kashiprosad Ghose is also counted as one of the key pillars of indo-Anglian literature. His contribution in Indian literature in English is as equivalent as Henry Derozio. His *The Shair and Other Poems* finds a place in literary Indian history. Even he is considered as the first Indian to publish a regular volume of English poetry. Ghose edited an English weekly The Hindu Intelligence. His poems are counted as didactic as good touch of originality and conventional descriptions. Michael Madhusudan Dutta began writing while he was at Hindu College. He got numerous scholarships in college exams as well as a gold medal for an essay on women education. While a student his poems in Bengali and English were published in *Jnananvesan,* Bengal *Spectator, literary Gleamer, Calcutta Library Gazette, Literary Blossom and Comet,* at Hindu College. Lord Byron was Madhusudan's motivation. He was the first to use blank verse in 1860 in the play *Padmavati* based on a Greek legend. His next poems silenced the critics and detractors, and eternally established the trend of blank verse in literature. Madhusudan's epic poem: *Meghnad-Badh Kavya* is considered as his all-time magnum opus till today. Written in blank verse, this epic was based on the *Ramayana* but motivated by Milton's *Paradise Lost.*

Madhusudan changed the villainous Ravan into a Hero. This magnificent heroic-tragic epic was written in nine cantos which is quite exclusive in the history of Bengali Poetry. Meghnad-Badh Kavya was literature's first original epic in Bengali and gave Madhusudan the position of an Epic Poet. He fell utterly into debts and asked for help to the great personality, the scholar, social reformer, and protester Ishwarchandra Vidyasagar. His excessive life-style, uncertainty in money matters, and careless drinking to drown problems conspired to wreck his health and happiness, and similarly the health and happiness of his partner Henrietta, who had also drawn to alcoholism during her days of poverty in Versailles. To his courageous will, Bengali Literature owes its first blank verse and the sonnet, its first modern comedy and tragedy, and its first epic. Dutt was mainly inspired by the life and work of the English Romantic poet Byron. Madhusudan was a gifted as multilingual person. He was well versed in classical languages like Greek and Latin, besides Indian languages like Bengali, Sanskrit and Tamil. He also had a smooth understanding of languages like Italian and French and could read and write the last two with perfect grace and ease. Bengal was epicenter for renaissance as it has given literary scholars who gave reputation to mother India in the world. Amongst them, Toru Dutt is the first poetess in Indo-Anglian literature. She had English education and had a wealthy and respectable heritage. In 1875, she had translated French writing into English with the title *A Sheaf Gleamed in French Fields*. She had translated *Ramayana*, *Mahabharata* and *Sakuntala* into English verse too.

Another luminous star of Indian literature is Manmohan Ghose. He was an elder brother of Sri Aurobindo. His first poem collection – Primavera (1890) was valued by literary scholars and classmate at Oxford. Like Derizio, Manmohan Ghose became professor of English at the Presidency College, Kolkata. In 1898, he published set of poems – *Love Songs and Elegies and also wrote five act play- Perseus the Deliverer.* His poems were considered much intellectual thoughts and rhythm is dazzling feature. Manmohan Ghose's poetry in many ways broke with the earlier school of Orientalist poetry. His poems frequently spoke of a desire to return to England, where he had spent 22 years of his life. While his Indian contemporaries, including his brother Aurobindo Ghose, were writing on patriotic themes and were sketch upon ancient Indian culture, Manmohan Ghose turned to England for encouragement. Up to this time, Indian literature had flourished in full bloom but it was Rabindranath Tagore who brought Indian literature at world level and achieved for modern India, a place on the world literary history that won Noble Prize for literature and gave identification to India on global scale. Rabindranath Tagore the multitalented personality of Indian literary scholar is considered as – the Gurudev, the Rishi and the Maharshi. He was a poet, dramatist, actor, producer, musician, artist, an educationist, reformer, thinker, telepathist, novelist, story writer, and a critic of life and literature. Rabindranath Tagore wrote mostly in Bengali and translated many of his poems and plays into English. For *Gitanjali* (1912) he won the Noble Prize for literature and became poet of the world. After this, his other works and *Gitanjali* were translated by literary writers into major languages of world. To his glory, there is a long list of poems and plays, both in Bengali and English which had made his place amongst the greatest writers of the world. In Iyengar's words:

> As the years passed, he became more and more a legendary figure; in his flowing bead and immaculate white robes he was truly in the line of the great Rishi of Upnishadic times, and indeed he was truly in the line of the great bearing witness to the triune Reality, seeing the way showing it to others.[2] *(Iyengar: 1995, 103)*

The productive soil of Bengal has given a twinkling hero to the world in the figure of Sri Aurobindo Ghose. He is the one of the uncontestable great figures in Indo-Anglian literature. He had contributed much to Indian literature and also lifted his works at globe. Sri Aurobindo's long poetic journey has given him the height of literary master of Indo-Anglian literature. His *Songs to Myrtilla* and longer poems of the early period- *Urvasie* were available in 1895 and 1896 respectively. The most wonderful work of Indo-Anglian literature is his *Savitri* which is in three parts, divided in to xii cantos which have total 23813 lines, on which the poet worked for fifty years of his life. M.K. Naik observes in *A History of Indian English Literature* that;

> *Savitri* was continuously revised by the poet almost till the end of his days and shaped into an epic of humanity and divinity, of death and the life divine. A sort of poetic philosophy of the spirit and of life, and an experiment in mystic poetry cast in to a symbolic figure [3] (M.K. Naik: 1995, 52).

In the list of the pioneers for Indo-Anglian literature, Sarojini Naidu was the first feminine contributor who served Indo-Anglian literature for her life time. She was versatile personality and more than a poet as she had occupied some of the highest official positions in the society of India. Her first volume of poetry *The Golden Threshold* (1905) was followed by *The Bird of Time* (1912) and *The Broken Wing* (1917) made her greatest poetess of the era. Her lyrics have a perfect structure and a superb finish and she handles various meters and stanza forms in her poem rightly. M.K. Naik observes;

> Her best poetry is not just a faded eco of the feeble voice of Decadent romanticism, but an authentic Indian English lyric utterance exquisitely tuned to the composite Indian ethos, bringing home to the unbiased reader all the opulence, pageantry and charm of traditional Indian life, and the splendors of the Indian scene.[4] (M.K.Naik:1995,69)

The significance of Gandhi in Indo-Anglian literature is

exceptional as he has prepared a new generation of literature which later came to be familiar with as Gandhian literature. Mahatma Gandhi himself was neither a writer nor he was so eager in the art of writing but he had influenced much to people of India and at globe also. The period between the two world wars and comprising them both was the Indian Gandhiyan Age. He has touched every part of our national life – economical, political educational, religious, social life and the language and literature. Gandhiji has influenced our languages and literatures not only directly but also indirectly. In the social globe, the Gandhian movement led to deletion of untouchability, awakening among women, religious transformation movements, awakening amongst the depressed classes etc. which has deeply influenced Indian literature in English. His autobiography- *Experiments with Truth* (1925) which describes the unfolding process is one of the everlasting classics of Indian literature. His writings can be divided in to three periods as:

(1) The Early London Period (1888-1891)

(2) The South African Period (1893-1915)

(3) The thirty three years of the Indian Period (1915-1948).

Among the writings of Gandhi, his autobiography *My Experiments with Truth* is the most marvelous work. Mahatma Gandhi's writing unfolds social, political, cultural, ethical and spiritual issues. His writing has intense openness which has attracted millions of readers and recognized itself as Gandhian literature. Jawaharlal Nehru is the most noteworthy name in the history of India as well as in the history of Indo-Anglian literature. He was the true recipient of Gandhi in politics and one in the greatest leaders of Indian independence. His first book-*Soviet Russia* is the set of articles where Nehru views Russia as India's admirer and strong supporter for the progress. His first collection of letters published as-*Letters from a Father to His Daughter*

(1930) consists of thirty one letters written by him to his daughter Indira Gandhi. His most notable work-*Glimpses of World History* is written between October 1930 and august 1933 comprising the 196 letters written by Nehru in jail. This book is examination of world history from the beginning of civilization to mid 19th Century. *An Autobiography* is literary success of Nehru as writer. It is also live record of moments of Indian History for well over a generation, present epoch and strong sense of history. In the words of M.K. Naik;

> Nevertheless, by virtue of its sincerity and vividness and its Manifest historical and literary importance, the work indubitably ranks among the major autobiographies in world literature.[5] (M.K. Naik: 1995, 129)

Up to the time of Jawaharlal Nehru, the Indo-Anglian literature blossomed and spread its beauty at the globe. It is also vital to cite that the literary genre-prose and poetry flourished at its height in India but novel a new literary form yet to grow on the Indian land by the master novelists.

The researcher would like to search the rise of novel in India and the initiator fathers of novel where it ripen in the hands of trio – Mulk Raj Anand, R.K. Narayan and Raja Rao. It is very much apparent that novel form of literature was new for India but it has been easily

accepted by Indian English writers as well as by writers of regional languages. The truth that Indian literatures are a result of a multilingual, multicultural, and socio–historical blend cannot be ignored. In case of Indian literature, it can be said that it presents the single thought written in many languages. Though it is not possible to neglect the criticism uttered by a few critics who do not entirely agree to the concept of a common family of Indian languages or common culture necessarily determining the singleness or harmony of literatures in India, serious thought is given to the essential oneness underlying Indian literatures. In Indian literature, other forms of literature were quite old as their fundamentals were laid down centuries back but the 'novel' as literary type was latest to India. Poetry, epics, drama, short stories and fables have their old literary record. 'Novel' was actually the last to appear on the Indian English literary scene. It was only during a period of slight more than a century that the novel-the long maintain piece of prose fiction-has crop up and taken origin in India.

At primary level, the Indian novel in English has been reflected upon explored and analyzed from the viewpoint of history and historiography, genus and language, 'Indianness' and Indian awareness with the majority of critics date its beginning back to the mid 19th century when the Bengali writer Bankimchandra Chatterjee published his *Raj Mohan's Wife*. In India, the beginning of the modern novel as a realistic depiction of Indian human in society and relating back to the European genre as it had evolve from the eighteenth century onward has been dated back to the late second decades of the twentieth century. In the second half of the 19th century, stray novels continued to emerge mostly by writers from the Bengal, Madras and Mumbai. A majority of these novels are social and historical, and their models are visibly the 18th and 19th century British narrative, particularly Defoe, Fielding and Scott. An attractive development is the astonishingly early appearance of women novelists. After the end of the First World War it was found that some of the novelists were influenced by the ideologies that challenged capitalism and colonialism. In Mulk Raj Anand's novels we find the operation of the principles in the backdrop. His *Across the Black Waters, Coolie, Two Leaves and a Bud, Untouchable* are faithful documents of the lives of the oppressed. His characters also come alive as real persons of the Indian society. Among other novelist, Raja Rao is well-known for his narrative techniques. He collective the narrative techniques of *Ramayana* and *Mahabharata* with those modern western techniques of Eliot and Joyce. His *Kanthapura* is put in the mouth of a grandmother. R. K. Narayan is a dominant novelist having considerable philosophical bent of mind. It is seen in his novels *The Bachelor of Arts and The Dark Room.* Khushwant Singh wrote *A Train to Pakistan.* His next novel *I Shall Not Hear the Nightingale* presents a sarcastic picture of a Sikh family, illustrative of different Indian reactions to the freedom movement of the forties. Actually, the partition theme in Indian English novels set the dystopian tune, which would be later on carried on to the tone of the postcolonial theories. Post colonialism began as recognition of the leading post-war economic and political conditions existing all over globe.

Today, the Indian novelists in English are large in number. Besides Mulk Raj Anand, R.K. Narayan and RajaRao, the three principal Indian writers of English fiction, Besides, also K. Nagrajan, Bhabhani Bhattacharya, Manohar Malgonkar, Khushwant Singh, Shashi Deshpande, Kamla Markandya, Anita Desai, Amitav Ghose and many more. All these novelists have extensively enhanced Indian literature. Among these writers, the most famous is Salman Rushdie, born in India, now living in the United Kingdom. Rushdie with his famous work *Midnight's Children* ushered in a new style of writing. He used an amalgam language – English liberally infused with Indian terms – to convey a theme that could be seen as representing the vast picture of India. He is regularly categorized under the magic pragmatism mode of writing most famously linked with Gabriel Garcia Marquez. Bharati Mukherjee, author of *Jasmine,* has spent much of her career exploring issues relating immigration and identity with a particular focus upon the U.S.A. and Canada. Vikram Seth, author of *A Suitable Boy* (1994) is an author who uses a clean English and more realistic themes. Being a self-confessed fan of Jane Austen, his attention is on the story, its details and its twists and turns. Shashi Tharoor, in his *The Great Indian Novel,* pursues a story-telling style as in the Mahabharata drawing his ideas by going back and forth in time. Other writers include, Kiran Desai, Chitra Banerjee Divakaruni, Raj *Kamal* Jha, Jhumpa Lahiri, Bharti Kirchner, Amit Chaudhuri, Vikas Swarup, Rohinton Mistry, Kiran Nagarkar and C R Krishnan, Chetan Bhagat. These days, Indian literature reached at the top of creation with the contributions of regional and national writers. The recent development in Indian literature is most notable in the history of Indian English literature. The novel by Arundhathi Roy – *The God of Small Things* (1997) won the Booker Prize. The book has brought attention of readers from every country and made Indian literature indistinguishable at internationally. This work is considered as a chief contribution to Indian literature. The Indian novels in English not from its beginnings but from about the time K.S. Venkataramani's *Murugan, The Tiller* and *Kandan, The Patriot* considered the opening period. Both of these novels have been usually acknowledged as the first 'Modern' Indian novels written in English because of their writer's concern with pressing contemporary political and social matters and their more pragmatic production. The novel ends with Ramu's origin of an ideal rural colony on Gandhian principles. In Indian, the social life is totally illustrated with vagaries and varieties that the novelist with a sharp-eye and a sympathetic heart will find the material spread out before him to be literary inexhaustible. It is also notable that the theme and method of novels in Indian literature through this period found based on social disturb, dearth, untouchability, exploitation, social and political movement etcetera. Iyengar observes;

> Some of the best studies of social life are, naturally enough, in the regional languages; and it is not easy to translate the racy idioms of every day speech into English. This is particularly true of life in the countryside, the seaside, the hillside

> where life has, perhaps, changed very little indeed during the last two thousand years. Urban life in India attracts the novelist by its excitements, perversions, sophistications and violent alternations between affluence and poverty, splendor and squalor; but the interior, the areas of obscurity and inaccessibility have their attractions too and sometimes bring out the best in the creative novelist.[6] (*Iyengar: 1995, 327)*

The history of Indian literature in English has most striking event in the nineteen thirties, appeared on the scene of its major trio; Mulk Raj Anand, R. K. Narayan and Raja Rao, whose first novels were published in 1935, 1935 and 1938 respectively; and it is a mark of their figure that they uncovered each in his own typical way, the various possibilities of Indian English novels.

2

Literary Canon

Researching how literature is formed and testing claims for its place in the canon makes us greater readers. In lieu of stopping at 'I like it' or 'I do not', readers will be able to speak about what 'it is' and what kinds of attractive or unattractive effects it creates. This process assists in canon formation. The term 'literary canon' refers to a categorization of literature. It is a phrase used broadly to refer to a set of literary works that are considered the most significant of a particular time period or place. For instance, there can be a literary canon comprised of works from a particular country, or works written in a specific time or even a collected works that were all written during a specific time span and within a certain region. In this way, a literary canon sets a collection of similar or related literary works. There are many ways in which literary works can be categorized, but the literary canon seems to affect a certain authority to a work of literature. When a work is entered the canon, thus canonized, it gains status as an official adding up into a group of literary works that are widely studied and valued. Those who decide whether a work will be canonized comprise significant literary critics, scholars, teachers, and anyone whose opinions and judgments regarding a literary work are also broadly respected. As a result, there are no strict qualifications for canonization, and whether a work will be canonized remains a personal decision. Literary canons, like the works that include them and the judgments of those who create them, are continuously changing. Literature is affected by the experiences and feelings of writers and readers. So, Literature changes in the context of shifting experience and thought. This context is most important to the framework of a literary canon. More often than not, it is those works that are considered contextually significant that achieve entry into the canon. This means that the literary work is relevant to constant trends or movements in thought and art, or speak to to historical or current events, etc. Anyone who has studied literature in a school or university in the western world knows what that suggests. It means that the works in the canon get read, read by trainee students and apparently specialist teachers. It also means that to read these honored works is a privilege and a symbol of privilege. It is also a sign that a person has been canonized himself -- beatified by the experience of being introduced to beauty, admitted to the ranks of those of the internal circle that are familiar with the canon and can judge what belongs and does not.

This canon limits the trainee reader far more than the trainer, for few students have time to read afar the reading list. Indeed, few know that one can read beyond it since what lies beyond is by defining tedious, darkened, and dreary. One must not exaggerate the inflexibility of the canon, since the works that are included continuously change. Emphasizing that writers enter and leave the canon or shift their virtual position within it takes away little from its power. One can appear at this power of the canonized work in two ways. Gaining entrance evidently allows a work to be enjoyed; failing to do so thrusts it into the midpoint of the unobserved, unread, un-enjoyed, and un-existing. In other words, Canonization permits the member of the canon to be read and therefore not only live but also be immortalized. Like the picture accepted as a painting and not, say, a mere decorative object or even paint spill, it receives a theoretical frame, and although one can remark upon the apparent facts that frames confine and fraction, precisely such look within the frame guarantees its artistic study its capacity to make the observer respect it, take it with respect. In addition to promoting this sort of falsification that misguide us about the works inside it, a canon has an even more severe effect on those works left out: if belonging to the canon brings a work to notice, thrusts one into view, falling out of it or being not present, exiled from it keeps a poem or novel out of it. It is in effect excommunicated. Likewise, one of the most sober results of not belonging to the canon is that these works do not converse with one another. A work without the canon is forgotten, unnoticed, and if a canonical author is under debate, any links between the non canonical work and the canonical tend to be unnoticed.

However, under certain conditions, non canonical works can come into view at the other end of the connections. But such connections and such linkages to the canonical need almost heroic and certainly particular hard work. The typical intelligent educated reader, in other words, is not likely to be able to make such connections with the non canonical work. For them they do not exist. The connections are made among specific works and by those readers – professionalized by the scholars – whose job it is to explore the reader's equal to darkest Africa of the19th and early 20th century imagination – the darkest stacks of the records where dwell the irrelevant, unnoticed books, those one is supposed not to know, not even to have seen. The situation not so strangely resembles that of the unknown Dark Continent which surely was not dark or unknown to itself or to its inhabitants but only to Europeans who tagged it so because to them, from their vantage point, it was out of view and insight. They did so for obviously political – indeed, actually colonialist – reasons, and indeed one may question if this isolated, divided placement at a distance exactly figures the political economy of works canonized and non- canonized. It has been debated that until a literature has a 'canon,' it has not risen to the level of superiority at which it can be studied sincerely by the elite. Scholarly study creates canons by making accurate texts available and by showing the terms by which they are studied. For instance, folk literatures likely not to have canons until scholars have got into the act, collecting and relating and analyzing the wild oral televise of the folk tale or song. People may argue whether Tune X is really a blues song rather than rock and roll or rhythm and blues, but until a canon of 'blues' is present, people will tend to disagree rather hopelessly about the facts. When asked whether Tune X is a great blues song, their views will be even more separated by appeals to unsteady definitions until people have taken the time to make serious, methodical studies of the how the art is shaped. Canonization also distorts literature and introduces projected bias in analysis. Canons of literature may freeze their subject and lessen its study to dry memorization for its own sake. The rules, by which the canonical texts are elected, are tend to be favored the powerful and to exclude or marginalize the ineffective, regardless of the merits of their work. Or, rather, 'merit' will become instinctively recognized as a property 'naturally' belonging to the powerful, and 'naturally' engaged to the powerless. The values and tastes of the powerful will turn the process of canon formation and its product into a cultural bondage. One also can argue that canons and the scholarship which produced are not good for literatures, themselves, and that those habits of intense examination and careful explanation can produce a kind of self-awareness that will kill poets' creative energy and the empathic appreciation of their viewers. Scholarship which respects the secrecy in poets' minds and the essential role of emotional affect in audiences' responses, even while it tries to learn more about how literature works, is the only kind worth pursuing. Imaginative writers should look for stimulation in the practices of early writers where they will find lost techniques and elapsed subjects they can bring to new life in their own work. All readers should listen silently for the heartbeat of these early works, hidden from us by our unfamiliarity with their terms and the rules by which they play the poets' playoffs.

Thus, belonging to the canon confers status, social, political, economic, artistic, none of them can easily be extricated from the others. Belonging to the canon is a guarantee of excellence, and that guarantee of high artistic quality serves as a promise, a contract, that announces to the viewer, it is heard that -purpose, Complex, difficult, privileged, the object before you have been winnowed by the sensitive few and the not-so-sensitive many, and it will refund your attention. You will receive pleasure; at least you are supposed to, and if you don't, well, perhaps there is something off with your apparatus. Such a declaration of status by the poem, painting, or building, masterpiece, or dance that has appeared ensconced within a canon serves a powerful separating purpose: it instantly stands forward, different, better, to be valued, loved, and enjoyed. It is the wheat winnowed from the chaff, the rare survivor, and it has all the privileges of such survival.

FOLK-ORAL WRITING

One of the most fundamental developments in this century in both the popular and intellectual understanding of culture has been the wide growth of awareness that only a little percentage of man's total creativity has depended on literacy. Writing is at most a comparatively recent awkward innovation, and while it is useful for keeping records of all sorts, it is a futile means of cultural communication, even with the help of printing. In spite of their mechanical awkwardness and inadequacy, writing and printing are indisputably two great tools of civilization. But they are not basic assets of human nature. The more primary and most distinguishing cultural property of men everywhere remains their instinctive power of speech. Spoken words are the ultimate source of graphic communication, and any decay or reduction of the arts of speech at once erodes the value of vivid culture. We live in an age when, moreover, other potentially humanizing inventions based on electrical recording and electrical spreading of speech has only begun to be used and respected. A large part of current speech in any language is temporary, and is employed for merely momentary purposes. But a certain proportion of spoken communication is continuing, whether or not any record is made of it in writing or otherwise. It expresses ideas of such a verified, lasting utility that special, *poetic* modes of speech are present in every language to assure the remembrance and continuation of those vital ideas in *oral traditions*. *Oral literature* is the objects recorded from oral civilization in every age and in every language.

Folk oral literature:

The figures of oral works, equally in verse and prose, which are produced usually by anonymous writers and are preserved in the people's mind for a long time by being passed on orally from one generation to other. Ukrainian folk oral literature has its unique artistic qualities, its unique poetic devices—metaphors, similes, epithets, and symbolism. The poetic folk literature consists generally of folk songs, which are subdivided into various forms: ritual songs -songs related with spring rituals, with vesnianky-hahilky, carols, shchedrivky, Kupalo festival songs, harvest songs, wedding songs and funeral songs-, historical songs and Dumas, lyrical songs and dance songs. Folk prose can be divided into fables, fairy tales, stories, legends, anecdotes, and so on. Poetic-prose folk literature is related to spells, proverbs, sayings, and riddles. In the nineteenth century, the mechanism of folk oral literature was held to be the products of a collective popular mind. Contemporary folklorists support the hypothesis that individuals are the creators of the oral tradition. However, in the basic examples of ancient folk oral literature, the words are connected with ritual actions and the oral text and ritual events always have a realistic, vital purpose. This delimits the creative desire of the performer. The fundamental changes that occur in the works of the oral practice are caused by their dissociation from the original ritual contexts in which they arose. The orally conveyed image that is separated from the ritual, loses its original practical inspiration and becomes forgotten or else acquires a new motivation, becomes accepted, and begins a fresh life. Hence, with the coming of Christianity and the church's refusal of folk literature and folk customs and rites as pagan relics, folk oral literature, however, managed to hold its vivacity and to attract the influences of medieval written literature. Already commencement with the Renaissance, there was a steady exchange between oral and written literature. Miscellaneous folklore-literary forms of the baroque appeared—for instance, the interludes, through which Christmas, Easter, ironic, and parodic verse passed into folklore. The populist movement of the nineteenth century declared folk oral tradition as the rule and canon for all literature, while literature of the nineteenth and the beginning of the twentieth century methodically grew closer to the folk roots by engrossing certain elements of the language, genres, and content of the folk tradition.

The chief genres of conventional folk literature continued to exist under the Soviet rule. After decades in which the Soviets struggled against certain forms of folk oral literature that were viewed as 'religious vestiges' and tried to create synthetically a pseudo Soviet folklore, the old carols, spring songs, Easter songs, harvest songs, and wedding songs continued to form the most vital part of the oral literature among the peasantry of the collective farms. They were also boosted by the nationally conscious intelligentsia. The Soviet authorities tried to take advantage of this fact in creating so-called Soviet rites, usually by replacing old lyrical songs with new ones dealing mostly with life on the collective farm or in the developed city. The so-called 'Soviet folklore' was controlled to such themes as the glorification of Vladimir Lenin and the Communist Party, the construction of communism, the victories of the Soviet Army, and the heroes of labor. A good deal of attention was dedicated in Soviet publications on folklore to 'antireligious folk literature.' The same was true of the rich folk materials that were created in the jails and concentration camps of the Union of Soviet Socialist Republics.

SANSKRIT LITERATURE

The earliest works of literature in India were orally transmitted. Sanskrit literature begins with the *Rig Veda* a collection of holy hymns dating to the period 1500–1200 BCE. The Sanskrit epics *Ramayana* and *Mahabharata* came on the stage towards the end of the first millennium. Classical Sanskrit literature came out in the first few centuries of the first millennium. In the medieval period, literature in Kannada and Telugu appeared in the fifth and eleventh centuries respectively. Then after, literature in Marathi, Bengali, and various dialects of Hindi, Persian and Urdu began to emerge as well. The renowned poet and playwright Kālidāsa wrote two epics: *Raghuvamsha* – Dynasty of Raghu and *Kumarasambhava* – Birth of Kumar Kartikeya; they were written in Classical Sanskrit rather than Epic Sanskrit. Other instances of works written in Classical Sanskrit include the Pāṇini's *Ashtadhyayi* which standardized the

grammar and phonetics of typical Sanskrit. The Laws of Manu is an important text in Hinduism. Kalidasa is often considered to be the greatest writer in Sanskrit literature and one of the supreme poets in Sanskrit, whose *Recognition of Shakuntala* and *Meghaduuta* are the most famed Sanskrit dramas. He occupies the same place in Sanskrit literature that Shakespeare occupies in English literature. Some other famous dramas were *Mricchakatika* by Shudraka, *Svapna Vasavadattam* by Bhasa, and *Ratnavali* by Sri Harsha. Later poetic works include *Geeta Govinda* by Jayadeva. Some other famous works are Chanakya's *Arthashastra* and Vatsyayana's *Kamasutra.*

The most outstanding Prakrit languages were the Jain Prakrit (Ardhamagadhi), Pali, Maharashtri and Shauraseni. One of the earliest existing Prakrit works is Hāla's album of poems in Maharashtri, the Gāhā Sattasaī, dating to the third to fifth century CE. Kālidāsa and Harsha also used Maharashtri in some of their drama and poems. In Jainism, many Svetambara works were written in Maharashtri. Many of Aśvaghoṣa's plays were written in Shauraseni as were a sizable number of Jain works and Rajasekhara's *Karpuramanjari.* Canto thirteenth of the Bhaṭṭikāvya is written in what is called 'like the vernacular' (bhāṣāsama), that is, it can be read in two languages at the same time: Prakrit and Sanskrit.

3

Role of Prakrit Literature to Indian Literature

It is essential to know the exact status of Prakrit among the available stock of twenty hundred languages of the world divided into twelve major families. The Indo-European is a major family amongst them. The Indo-Aryan constitutes a major branch of the Indo-European family. The Indo-Aryan family is, in comparison with Sanskrit, the educated and cultured class generally identified a little of Prakrit languages. The ever-flowing stream of human being subdivided and titles as Old, Middle and New. Besides the Vedic as a literary language, many regional languages were prevailing among the common people. George Griersson in his Linguistic Survey of India has referred to all spoken or conversational languages during and before the Vedic period as Primary Prakrits. Even if various dialects and sub-dialects were engaged to bring out day to day requirements of an ordianary people, it took several centuries for Prakrit to presume a form of literary language. Particularly it was when Mahaveer and Buddha adopted Ardhamagadhi and Pali respectively as language of religious sermons, we find the sunrise of literature in these languages. For many centuries there was a delusion that 'Prakriti' means 'Sanskrit' and those who could not utter it properly, resorted to impure Sanskrit i.e. Prakrit. It was a Jain author Namisadhu who first gave the clarification of the word 'Prakrit' very logically. He said, 'Prakriti' is 'nature'.

Prakrits are natural and spontaneous expressions of people devoid of firm rules of grammar etcetera. These natural languages were lucid to women, children and uneducated commoners. The word Prakrit stands for a group of languages and does not refer to any individual language. Marathi, Bengali, Orisa, Assamese, Bihari, Hindi, Gujrati, Rajastani, Marwadi, Punjabi, Sindhi, Kashmiri are all the varieties of new or modern Indo-Aryan languages. All these regional languages are developed from their respective varieties of Prakrits -technically called Apabhramsha- and not directly from Sanskrit. The Dravidian languages ,Tamil, Telugu etc., and Tribal languages are of course not integrated in the Indo-Aryan languages and as a result they do not possess their respect Prakrit varieties. Jain Maharashtri is a language-variety created and used in vast narrative and biographical literature by Jain writer.

This peculiar language was understandable to the people residing Maharashtra, Gujrata, Madhyapradesha, Uttarapradesha and Rajastana for nearly one thousand years. Svetambara Jain Acharyas formed religious, philosophical moralistic literature in various literary forms that is- narratives, biographies, legendary histories, epics, eulogies etc.

All the above mentioned languages developed linguistic changes by tenth century A.D. and gave rise to Apabhramsha languages. Prakrit showed a different picture of society and culture from the Sanskrit literature. It is a broad picture of social and cultural aspects of the people, not simply of the 'naagara' or elite class. The heroes and heroines belong to the middle class of the society e.g. goldsmiths, coppersmiths, potters, weavers, confectioners, fisherman, merchants, monks, nuns, courtesans, middle-class and low-class housewives, merchants, thieves, beggars and so on. This literature signify the festival, celebrations, fares, religious gatherings, clubs, vows and rituals, pilgrims, food-offerings, customs and beliefs of the common people of the society. Really the realistic picture of the society helps us to grasp the true Indian aspirations

4

After Amnesia, 'Of Many Heroes

A dominated culture learns not just to be like the culture that dominates it, but also tries to cover its own surroundings. In such cultural encounters, amnesia plays the most important role in defining the self-perception of cultures. G. N. Devy's *After Amnesia*, first published in 1992, offers an keen study of contemporary literary scholarship in Indian languages by indicating how modern Indian languages 'learnt to forget' that literary criticism had been discarded by them during the post-Sanskrit medieval centuries, and how they have posed before themselves a false choice of scholar practices fixed in culturally distant Western or Sanskrit traditions. *After Amnesia* proposes that what has come to be seen as a disaster in Indian literary criticism can be understood if a related historiography is generated. '*Of Many Heroes*', first published in 1997, is an effort to formulate such a historiography. If *After Amnesia* is an essay on literary criticism, '*Of Many Heroes*' is a historiography of literary historiography in India. It presents a wide range of survey of texts on literary history, beginning with the fourth century Bhartrihari's *Vakyapadiya* to the seminal texts created during the twentieth century. The Reader brings together two other new essays by G. N. Devy – *The Being of Bhasha* and *Countering Violence*. These philosophical essays discuss the importance of dialects and vanishing languages in the making of civilized culture, the place of silence and lunacy in the making of meaning, and of language itself in the future of knowledge. After closely analyzing the sociological and psychological roots of cruelty, the writer argues that the growing violence in modern societies and the loss of languages in an increasingly prejudiced and aggressive world require to be seen as closely related aspects of the cultural impact of historical processes germinating in colonialism and globalization against cultural plurality. The four essays simultaneously present a complete theory of knowledge in postcolonial times. They present a request for a radical reorientation to the question of education, knowledge, expression and analysis of linguistic creative.They are, perhaps, the most challenging and unconventional theory on epistemic and hermeneutical issues central to modern Indian culture. A literary scholar and cultural advocate, G. N. Devy writes in three languages – Marathi, Gujarati and English, and has received prominent literary awards for his works in all the above three languages. His academic and activist work shows a rare mixture of a deep interest in India's classical literature and philosophy, as well as the exposed languages of Adivasi and wandering communities, in higher education and rural development. To see Ganesh Devy as a noun is boring. This makes him sound like a conventional professor, a professional literary critic, a concerned activist. All this he is. But as a verb Ganesh Devy is much more appealing. He is a travelling friend, a collection of conversations and friendships. If Devy as a noun represents the official dictionary definition of Devy, as a verb Devy represents meaning in use. In a linguistic sense, he is the whole of his conversations with Mahasweta Devi, Bhupen Kakkar, Karan Grover, Dilip Chitre, A.K. Ramanujan and U.R. Ananthamurthy. It is out of these conversations that emerges another Devy, the Devy of thought experimentations, a Devy possessed with deconstructing supremacy. Hegemony is an odd term, both double-edged and Janus-faced, an ironic joke explaining why exploitation is so seductive. When Antonio Gramsci detailed it, it must have activated the occasional snigger in the isolation of prison life. Hegemony creates symbolic wounds we ought to to understand. It is not as simple as oppression or as brutal as pressure. It persuades, it convinces, it tricks like the witches in Macbeth, without the victim ever tracing the source of deceit. The irony about supremacy is that it deceives those who are supposed to see through it. It cons, in particular, the intellectual who practices the hermeneutics of disbelief.

An intellectual in India isn't merely twice born but double wounded. Symbolically, he suffers from colonialism and also the sins of progress. The violence of these events commands the need for a Freud or an Adorno. Yet one mourns the absence of a reliable local reading of colonialism. India lacks a Fanon or an Edward Said, someone who can split apart the supposed in authenticity of the wrongly classical and yet question the hypocrisy of the contemporary. We can, obviously, present an Ashish Nandy and celebrate his models of colonialism in terms of the sexuality of male and female and also adduce Gandhi as an answer. Gandhi fits the challenge to hegemony from such a structure. Later, Nandy created the opposition between myth and history arguing that symptoms of history are often a precursor of cruelty in our humanity. One thinks of the destruction of the Babri Mosque or the violent rhetoric of Narendra Modi in this context. Nandy, while playful, is often incomplete, a more happy-go-lucky cuckoo, laying his assumption like eggs waiting for some dull social science crow to formulate them. At another level, for all their agility, Nandy's essays still come out like a Freudian salad served up with limited dressing. Ganesh Devy realizes that such efforts are not complete. One needs a different canvas and the colors of a different palette. One requires a site beyond political economy, the world of infancy, or even the body. It is more self-evident, more primitive. It also demands a basic weakness, as the psychoanalyst becomes his own case study. In a cruel way, the intellectual's life becomes a lens and mirror to his own study, creating a vulnerability that leaves most challenges scarred and fragile. The intellectual appears like a cultural hunchback in his own note pads and he is forced to ask, 'I speak and write, therefore I wonder who I am.' In setting up the problematic, Devy implies that the Indian intellectual is a creature troubled by two doubles, the past as nostalgia and the present as development. By disfiguring and being disfigured by both, the thinker stands as a peculiar and pitiable creature. Steiner opines:

> Devy demands a double catharsis, insisting on creative therapies both for the past and the future for the present to become viable. It is like writing a drama twice, first, as a Greek tragedy with its sense of fate and second as a modern tragedy with its sense of choice. [7] (Steiner: 1963, 53)

Colonialism has a sense of Greek certainty possibly because of the past tense, while progress smacks of the modern, the possibility of choices. For Devy, both function within the logic of memory.

Devy's work is a search for the mnemonic man. It is an attempt to transfer memory and the original culture of memory as part of intellectual life. The idea of memory has to be released from its present meaning, its controlled codes and its ended ecosystem of imitation and seen for what it once was a cultural theory of creativity. To remember is to summon a space and to invent more possibilities for it. Memory isn't the Gutenberg memory of print where words are remembered by rote. Memory acquired the provinciality of print and became history or records. With print memory became automatic, acquiring the qualities of formula. No act of reading is possible without an alternative openness of memory. Devy's search for the mnemonic man begins with a try to look at amnesia and aphasia, as symptoms, as metaphors and as forms of life. Devy remarks:

> After Amnesia is an attempt to examine the collective memory of the intellectual in the colonial period.[8] (Devy: 2009, 45)

The scholar during colonial life felt that he was helpless and celebrated this fate as a mimic man. He was condemned to the second rate because he constructed himself as secondary to the colonial mind. The colonial meet was a corridor of mirrors without amusement. The Indian intellectual had no real contact to western thought and he adds to his impotence by severing access to his own context.

> He creates, in fact, a false imaginary fixing the great tradition of Sanskrit in amber and denying the everyday creativity of Bhasha.[9] (Devy: 2009,52-59)

He created a fake past by welding a fossilized concept of Sanskrit to a secondary notion of western literary criticism, freezing a society that was overflowing with a million celebrations of change. In celebrating Sanskrit and fossilizing it, he denied himself access to the Bhakti Movement. His scheme of criticism was secondary. He fixed, as it were, an ironic tourniquet, throttling the stream of the most creative juices of his society. Colonialism as an intellectual tragicomedy begins with the production of Sanskrit as an ideal past and the removal of Bhasha. In lieu of engaging with a Tukaram, Nanak or Kabir, it created idiot encounters between Shakespeare and Tulsidas, artificial engagements that never amounted to much. Colonialism hides its amnesia by creating a false encounter between the inauthenticity of an artificialized Sanskrit and the unavailability of the English thoughts. It was a coupling without organicity that the everyday-ness of Bhasha could have provided. The earliest past was isolated hermetically from the middle age and seen as depository of purist uniqueness. Literary critics museumized themselves in order to feel traditional. It was a odd kind of cultural virus which declared that what was authentically ours was second rate and secondary but what others saw as ours was seen as actual.

Second, what was once splendid was now read as dissolute and signs of decadence were read through an English literary sinology. Ideology became a self-inflicted disease where what was Indian was replaced by what was considered 'shiningly Indian'. It created false registers where western imperialism was seen as harmful but western literature was considered as great, thus denying the connections between the two. It was a double iatrogenic, where the patient first misreads the symptoms and goes one further by misreading the instruction. It created decades of mimic men whose genius lay in pursuing the secondary. Devy is not offering a monumental picture but showing how the power of leading trends was fatal. Colonialism, which was an intellectual scar, was read as a healing beginning. By lobotomizing a whole domain of time, Indian literary criticism lost the life-giving power of Bhasha, and its sense of native dynamics. It was like a river that was forced underground while a whole realm waited parched for the West. A society condemned to weakness needs its own rituals of coping. It creates an idea of a great past which turned decadent. Decadence allows for spoilage even as it evokes the forms of brilliance. It then seeks imitation as a proxy solace claiming access to the world of the dominated. It creates the rules of the second rate reducing the creativity of memory to rote. It thrives on little footnotes. Since it has denied itself originality, it creates new versions of it. The chase of the West as the Imperial, The Modern, and The Renaissance becomes the fresh triptych of culture. The rituals are simple. You wipe out your old self, imbibe a secondary other as a second-rate self and then ruin the margins with a fury, claiming they represent the field of non-knowledge. The 'other' outside is God, the 'other' within is an idiot and between hagiography and demonology, poorness lives content with itself. The modern Indian university system was an ode to this consciousness, a ritual devoted oxymoronically to the production and reproduction of incapacity.

The West was a spring that came in bottled containers. For the intellectual, the real and the creative were located in the West and the native museumized as either folklore or ancient. But it was a museumization of real life that was unjustifiable. The intellectual was consistently abject and repentant, embarrassed that a Meera, Tukaram or Kabir appeared like little fancy tokens before the power of British or Russian literature. He possessed an weakness that wished our past had a Shakespeare or a Dryden. It was an exorcism of the collective conscious where our symbols, memories were spring cleaned, to create a new discourse of the bhadrolok which relegated bhasha to the margins of folk or to foolishness or infancy. It was a destruction of a consciousness where the culture of the pre-British past was downgraded to the margins; a demolition of memory that hurts us even nowadays. It created a false proximity to a limited West and a distancing to one's own telepathic roots. It also twisted the Indian intellect which saw the West as prolific and India as secondary, such that colonialism launched a new cultural 'renaissance', itself a borrowed plumage, as revivalism.

Devy shows how this amnesia, the psychic disorder of a self-inflicted colonialism, moves across four stages of oppression, suppression, and depression. Cultural defeat makes us destroy our own past and acquire a sense of lowliness which then repeats that same violence on our margins seen as dialects, wanderers or tribes. Colonialism left behind the Trojan horse of development so that India could move from amnesia to aphasia, from erasure to speechlessness. If Devy were a Marxist he would say, history is invented twofold, first as amnesia, then as aphasia. Devy tells the story in twofold, first for the colony and then for the tribe. Here is a man, a literary critic obsessed with the fate of the tribe and the drifter. He realizes that the tribe and its oral culture have no place in literature considered as the domain of print. An oral literature is thought of as an oxymoron. Worse, the sociology of tribes is built either on a lack or a loss. Constructed in the language of progress, the tribe is semi-developed, savage, depressed, desperately in need of development. The savage has to be brought into history, with its availability of print and development. The rhetoric of lack and its technocratic strategies is accompanied by the parallel sentimentalism of loss, a sense of the artistic power of primitivism as art, as cosmology, as a mode of being in nature. As a fictional critic, Devy sees the tribe disappear between the savage tribe and the primitive tribe, lost as a past and unavailable to the future. Either way politics becomes a zero-sum game where the tribe is either assimilated or rubbed out. The tribe confronts either the liturgies of development or the litany of sorrow.

Devy realizes that politics cannot be reduced only to the politics of resistance. One cannot really fight the governing world and its discourses directly. One has to change its meanings. Autobiographically, he moves from literary censure to language. One needs both a new reading of science and another set of creation myths. He unfolds the complicity between western linguistics and western anthropology, arguing that language plays a different role in India from that conceptualized in western linguistic theory. Anthropology and linguistics share stereotypes by asserting that all literature is written. There is a genocidal politics implied in the theories. The written word acquires a totemic helplessness; the spoken word becomes banned. Devy has to challenge the established notion of literature as that which is written. As a first step, he seeks to create a revisionist ethnography which shows that the oral has its own forms of writing. He states the experiments of the Bondhali community, the Pithora paintings which are read as a form of writing, the Mahanubhav prose of the Chakardharas of thirteenth century North Maharashtra. In fact, he argues that, Whenever religious or social convention had to be challenged in India, new script traditions and new scripts had to be always employed as a means of struggle. But he realizes that ethnography by itself would have peculiarity, creating at best a tourist imprimatur, a Ripley's Believe it or Not around such areas. One needed not just a new ethnography of territory but also new policy of mapping.

Devy feels that the western understandings of linguistics created horror as a self-fulfilling insight. The death sentence is implied in the logic of assumptions. What linguistics and literary criticism in the West do is to segregate orality from literature by untying script and speech. The consequences are culturally disgusting. Consider a simple example. The linguistic survey and the government consider that there are only twenty-two languages in India. The rest are seen as dialects. Devy writes:

> Dialects are thus residually defined as all those languages without script. In an odd way, all the script less languages happen to be adivasi [10] (Devy: 2009, 11)

Devy argues that such a classification and its official consequences defy the creative logic of Indian traditions.

> Most of our linguistic creativity has been in the oral tradition. What developed in India as oral tradition was not just "writing" on walls and boards but also composition of texts, documents, or what one describes as "manuscripts". They follow the logic of speech not the logic of orthography.[11] (Devy: 2009, 10)

Devy then confronts the official terror imposed on the dialects, the violence inflicted on them by linguistic theory and the state, as a suppressor of dialects. Devy realizes that a sorority of bhasha as a cognitive domain, as a theory of survival places a different demand on cognitive politics. Neither Romanticism nor the pragmatic necessities of ethno-botany will be sufficient. To create a Rousseauian theory of education will appear too split.

The equation, the sibling ship between primitive and child can be misleading, reinforcing current stereotypes. Harlan Lane opines:

> One recognizes that the idea of the wolf boy produced fruitful theories of education for Maria Montessori but one needs a more deeply axiomatic theory.[12] (Harlan Lane: 1979, 120)

He argues that one needs a Meta narrative which is universal and a theory of culture that is playful. Devy locates in development the master text, the biological epic that one needs. Evolution is not a reductive biology but a describing, a primeval myth. Devy says:

> Evolution has two vehicles, two forms of expression. The first is the logic of body and the second centers around the fate of language [13] (Devy: 2009, 3)

According to Devy, the biological condition of having a spine is the primal act in this play. Standing up upright is an epic moment for 'man is the only human animal that stands perpendicular to the earth. All other creatures crawl, fly or swim.' The verticality of the spine has detached the brain far from the surface texture of the earth. Our direct experience of the earth is abridged in the process of development. It becomes mainly a conceptual understanding. This alienation from the earth creates two reflexes. Man both keeps viewing the world at a distance and looking at himself.

The spine forces us to reinvent our relation to our world; language likewise creates a basic reinventing of our relationship to the globe. It is language that permits a relationship to the external. Language, for Devy, is a puzzle covered in a mystery contained in a mystery. It is an indispensable movement of progression. Just as evolution provides for diversity at the genetic level, language provides for plurality at the cultural level. This creates two prime forms of theatre. There is at level alienation from the earth and using a corresponding meditation the creation of the 'other' by the mirroring of the self. Evolution, as play, demands a lighthearted relation to the 'other'. Within such an eye view, the drama of evolution is the drama of diversity, not the lessening of homogeneity. Monoculture is an uneducated interpretation of evolution. Once evolution is summoned as the new creation myth, its cosmicomics denies the dry picture called the survival of the fittest.

Once evolution becomes the meta-text, the next progress in cognitive political affairs opens. Devy's strategies are unconsciously similar to his colleague professional, A.K. Ramanujan. Ramanujan touches Devy's trajectory twice, once openly, once tacitly. Devy's first book, After Amnesia, is triggered by the title of Ramanujan's poems. As he confesses, the poignancy and poetry of the title outlasted the contents of the poem. But Ramanujan influences:

> Devy in a more generalized way. Playing Ekalavya to a more beneficent Drona, Devy adopts a similar style of questioning. In 1989, Ramanujan produced a wonderfully argumentative essay, 'Is There an Indian Way of Thinking? [14] (Ramanujan: 1989, 41-58)

His first progress is one of imitation. He tries to create a political economy of language a la Marx. There are shades of a Communist Manifesto for language in some of his early efforts uttered in terms of the same metaphorical claims. Instead of the hand mill giving us feudalism, and the steam engine capitalism, Devy feels that script was the first signal of free time and a device for the recognition and protection of spare. He recognized that many of his early formulations were both McLuhan like and immature. Talking to a seminar in Hyderabad he claimed,

> There is a direct correspondence between the deforestation of a country and the decline of the languages.[15] (Devy; 2009, 2)

In talking to his adivasi colleagues in 1997, Devy claimed that,

> The imagination is a capitalist invention, while memory is a criterion developed by communities that have not lost the ability for realism.[16] (Devy: 2009, 2)

Devy however realized that one needed more than rhetoric or the riposte of a hunch. One needed an architectonic of thought to create the possibility of a new cognitive commons. This demands a retelling of modes of relating to the world.

In a new preface to an adivasi what is called thinking, he differentiates four elemental modes: Truth and Revelation, Memory and Imagination. Once language becomes the medium, the amniotic, cognitive soup of Cultural Revolution, the human being has to locate him in space and time. Devy adds that, 'We control space through imagination and we control time through memory.'Consciousness is essentially a dream world, and it comes to terms with space and time through memory and the imagination. Without language, memory and time, there can be no fiction. Devy locates the locus of fiction at the connection of these three worlds. But for fiction to emerge it must be told. For storytelling to begin, it needs an act of otherness, to create the self as fantasy. Telling needs a 'not me', an 'otherness' for the social contract called listening to be born. If fiction needs language, memory and imagination, telling needs the presence of the other, the isolation between self and other that allows storytelling. The irony of memory is that it is a double-edged weapon. In an evolutionary sense, memory was used as a marker for dealings. Once transactions begin saving begins, capital pattern begins. Memory allows both for a surplus of capital and a propagation of stories. The basic purpose of the script was an act of numeracy, for counting. Devy argues that

> Scripts institutionalized greed and speech is threatened by scripts. The complicity between state and script is to control the story. This contract creates a form of suppression called aphasia [17] (Devy: 2009, 20)

Aphasia is the condition of muteness imposed by a state and its scripts on speech, on dialects, on orality. Once one defies state and script, both story and storytelling are reborn. If the first conflict was between memory and imagination, the second is between truth and exposure. Truth is a theology about what the consciousness fabricates. Truth tries to get at the limit of facts; revelation lies at the limit of fantasy. There was no one version of the truth in India. For some it was a linguistic creation, for others it arose from living out a world, for some truth was impossible without love. The linguists, the Bhakti poets, the Buddha and Gandhi, each selected for a different definition and the truthful life. This sense of the varieties of truth got lost in post-independence India. With independence, truth was not something to be kept within the confines of language or the universe of silence; it became a show. Its visuality demanded that it be shown. It had to be an image. The question of truth, of demonstrating truth in public, became a general problem. Imagine one was a tribal from India watching the Truth and Reconciliation Commission (TRC) in South Africa. Here the spectacle of truth was more important than the telling. There was an implied argument between telling lies and demonstrating the truth. The spectacle of the testimony became proof of the truth, where truth value lay in its visibility. Devy raises a deep point here. Many critics felt that the TRC was a great but faulty invention, and they located the flaw in the absence of compensation. The TRC examined a theory of truth and claimed it was unsatisfactory as a theory of justice. Devy tries to show that the TRC was incomplete even as a theory of truth. The idea of truth as spectacle vitiated the power of taletelling.

The TRC, when it began, was premised robotically on two ideas. It claimed that the idea of speaking the truth in public and being excused in public was a way to reconstitute the past as collective memory. Lucidity in the visual sense became innermost. Truth had been told in public, and then accepted. In the mold of visuality and archive fever, the possessiveness with the photograph and written document submerge the power of the story. What one created was a homogenization of memory as a language rather than a variety of the dialects of truth. This power of orality and substance of truth telling appeared during the Bhopal gas tragedy. For the victims, the memories of the disaster were seen as an oral commons of stories to be told and retold, lived and relived. For some of them, recompense was an act of print. In fact, compensation was an act of removal where the dialects of remembrance were to be erased through print, through the numeracy of numbers. Justice in Bhopal was an effort to repair the normalcy of civil service, the stability of contract and of print and property. It was the justice that literacy provides to a Gutenberg galaxy. Maybe this is why the victims invited the families working at the Union Carbide plant to visit them. They wanted to talk, listen and share stories. They wanted to build a commons of a memory through storytelling which could lead Gutenberg justice. One must stress that Devy does not an attempt to copy Marshall McLuhan. McLuhan showed sensitivity to technology and the ecologies it created. His was more an emphasis on the hearing and the auditory rather than the oral. For instance, he considered script as a part of literacy. His analysis of the transformations of the Catholic Church focuses more on the role of the microphone. The microphone, he claimed, created a new auditory community which ruined the old structure of the group.

However, There is reciprocity and a complementarily between the two. Edward remarks:

> One often feels that the failure of Holocaust museums lies in their visuality, in the need to reproduce the visual condition of the Holocaust [18] (Edward: 1995, 33)

Memory becomes a museum of visuality and looses the art of telling in company with its powers of silence. In a pole apart, one understands the logic of Hindi cinema as an amalgam of telling and the display. The rules of Hindi cinema are still located in the logic of oral cultures. The style of repeating a joke or story can be repetitive but it also appeals to a style of orality still present in the modern Hindi movie. There is mischievousness to Devy which he underplays in his stress on the political. This is implicit in the way he constructs modern thinking as a conversation of sickness of pathologies. Devy opines:

> A theory of knowledge is also a theory of the diseases that knowledge creates or suppresses. Implicit in the being of language is a theory of disease [19] (Devy: 2009, 14)

The question one asks plainly is: how do Devy's theories of literature and language add to his notion of democratic system. In fact, he explores the possibility of an independent evaluation of democracy. His is a search for how language and the idea of Bhasha can add to the imagination of democracy. Democracy in India is a bit like literary criticism. It claims the high ground and the Marg tradition. But sadly there is no desi, bhasha convention. In fact, the official canonical definitions of democracy blind one to the way people envisage, repeat, live and relive democracy as an everyday form of life. One never looks at Bhakti traditions of democracy as created in the lives of a Sunderlal Bahuguna, Baba Amte, Ela Bhatt and Mahasweta Devi. There is a different discussion and it shoots not from the Magna Carta or a theory of rights, but from the idea of democracy as a commons, as communities of speaking the dialects of the housewife, the tribe and the squatter. It is the latter who keep alive the bhasha theory of democracy, which sees democracy not as an import but a form of life native to the people.

The Bhasha theory, if I may call it that, does not look for voice and partaking. Voice which has no theory of speech is like a viewer who can never be a witness. He cannot tell a story. Democracy is a commons of memory; the vote is simply a marker of their memory. Memory needs retelling, reinvention, but the memory of the modern democracy reads more like the rote of print. Therefore, democracy becomes simply a memorial, a testament, rather than a lively form, whereas memory reinvents it in an everyday fashion. In that sense, the Bhasha theory of democracy is based not on the Guttenberg rule of law which look at the fine print but an orality of language which to modify Whitman's phrase sing -the body democratic. Devy hints that a technocratic theory of democracy is limited. A linguistic model of democracy which sees novelty in terms of an incalculable number of little variations, that infinity of diversities that both language and democracy demand, is what makes democracy sustainable. Equivalent to it is the idea of democracy as a sensorial. Modern democracy is often exceptionally visual, insisting on the spectacle and the magnificent. The visual gets entrapped in the gaze and the individual is often transformed into a specimen. Visuality, all too often, evokes the panoptical, the modes of inspection that have kept a polity orderly. What one needs instead is democracy as memory. Memory demands voice, the constant need for storytelling, and the nonstop hum of speech which pollinates a democracy. A democracy that allows for aphasia shuts up the diversities within it. Between the aphasia of the margins and the amnesia of the elite, democracy becomes a breakdown of storytelling, something which can neither be relived nor retold. The availability of the senses allows a democracy to take breaths, smell, hear and touch diversities as optional possibilities.

In appealing for a Bhasha theory of democracy, Devy sees democracy as a linguistic and literary sensibility, an oral enthusiasm. Frozen as a printed text, it becomes the domination of experts on development. Development is the internalization of poor standard where a culture imposes violence on the other because it can no longer bear itself. As a result, the experts on development are a bit like the old ideologists. They wipe out or lobotomize huge sections of what they call 'the third world' in us. The millions of DNTs, the forced migration of squatters, the displacement of dam projects, the unspecified removal of disaster victims, the thousands who vanish after a riot, the untold Africans within us, are all erased as non-people and non-knowledge. There is something impersonal about the bother of these essays. It is like a storyteller speaking in a separate way about extermination. There is no sentimentality, none of the usual mushiness of primitivism or the market sentimentalism of lost opportunities, no appeal to Utopia or profusion. This is no Cassandra cry, no Antigone living in the world of the dead. There is only a toast to life, the normalcy of the life world. What genocide cannot cope with is the silence of the living. The silence of the adivasi is Devy's constant mania. Anthropology cannot render as a garden what is a forest of stories. No print can capture the flight of speech. Silence refuses to be museumized. Devy's work is an attempt to create the poetics and politics out of the adivasi speech and stillness. Again, it needs to be listened to and sung all over.

5

The Bhakti Movement: Context and Overview

The Hindu tradition has commonly been separated into a number of important historical and religious periods through its long growth. The formative time period is highlighted by what are known as the holy texts, the Vedas, and a wandering people known as the Indo-Aryans; this period is classified as the Vedic Period. Central to the Vedas was the visionary figure of the rishi, or seer, one who was able to communicate with and about the various gods of the Vedic pantheon through a complex system of rituals that could only be performed by an progressively more powerful priesthood. Freedom was to be found through the precise performance of ritual.

The Epic and Classical Periods, from 400 BCE–600 CE are so given surnamed because of their focus on important texts, namely, the Mahabharata and the Ramayana. These epics are concerned with heroes and heroic deeds, kings, queens, and ideal roles of individuals. Also of central importance to this time frame were Law Books concerned with the ideal nature of society. Social order and stability were to be found in a hierarchical ordering of people over and above specific roles assigned to each individual's life stage (ashrama) and position in society (varna) or caste. On the upper step of this system was the Brahmin priesthood, followed by Kshatriyas (warriors) and Vaishyas (merchants), also known as two time-born classes. Only these groups were allowed to take part in a commencement ceremony known as the 'sacred thread', study the Vedas, and take part in Vedic rituals. Under these three groups were the Shudras, those were servants to the upper three Classes. Bottom this step came another subsection, the Untouchables, whose occupations were too polluting to succeed to fit within a controlled society. The way to liberation from rebirth or moksha was in a true understanding of religion, recognition and maintenance of the good of the social order, as exemplified and regulated by the Epics and Law Books.

In the medieval period, the Bhakti Movement was a very important aspect. This was due in part to the rise of a new line of kings, the Gupta lineage that supported the pantheon of gods through devotion of divine idols and also included the construction of temples and sustain for devotional groups. Together with these developments came a flourishing of mythical compositions about the gods, known as the Puranas, or, ancient stories. Central to this pantheon were the gods Vishnu, the cosmic king, and Shiva, the great yogi and ascetic known by many names, and his female counterpart, Shakti, or divine energy. Shakti was worshipped both as wife and wife of Shiva, but also in her own right as the Great Goddess in a variety of incarnations.

Most Hindus, today, recognize themselves with the worship of one of these gods. Devotees of Vishnu in his many forms—known as avatars, Krishna and Rama being the most popular Avtaars—are called Vaishnavites. Those worshiping Shiva are known as Shaivites, whereas followers of the feminine divine are Shaktas. Devotees within each thread focus on their god or goddess as Ultimate Reality, thus having a clearly monotheistic outlook, while at the same time acknowledging that the Divine takes many forms for the advantage of humanity. The term Bhakti is defined as -devotion, or passionate love for the Divine. Moksha, or liberation from rebirth, was not in the following of rules, regulations or communal ordering; it was through by simple devotion to the Divine. Within the movement at large, useful distinctions have been made by present-day scholars between those saint-poets who composed verses extolling God with attributes or form, namely, 'saguna' bhaktas, and, those extolling God without and beyond all attributes or form, 'nirguna.'

While the differences between these two branches are really important, their overarching similarities cannot be minimized; both focused on singular devotion, spiritual love for God, and had a particular focus on a personal correlation with the God. Given their faith in the centrality of personal devotion, poet-saints were highly critical of ritual observances as maintained and brought up by the Brahmins. For many, their criticism also included the caste system that supported the traditional religious chain, with Brahmins at the top of this hierarchy. Many saint-poets, particularly as the movement proceeded northward, were themselves of lower caste lineages. Another commonality was their usage of the dialect, or regional languages of the people, as different from the sacred language of the cream priesthood, Sanskrit. This practice, also, stemmed from the movement's focus on internal, mystical, and highly personal devotion to the Divine. Seminal Bhakti works in Bengali comprise the many songs of Ramprasad Sen. His pieces are identified as Shyama Sangeet. Coming from the seventeenth century, they cover an amazing range of emotional responses to Ma Kali, detailing philosophical statements based on Vedanta tradition and more intuitive pronouncements of his lovefor Devi. Using inventive metaphor, Ramprasad had 'dialogues' with the Mother Goddess throughout his poetry, at times chiding her, loving her, celebrating her as the Divine Mother, hasty consort of Shiva and capricious Shakti, the universal female creative energy, of the universe. Bhakti movement spawned into several different movements all across North and South India. Bhakti movement is nevertheless not differentiable by a Sufi movement of Shia Muslims of Chisti fame, In North India. People of Muslim faith adopted it as a Sufis while Hindus as Vaisanava Bhakti. Sufi saints of Chisti order produced first punjabi sufi saint named Baba Sheikh Farid Shakarganj, who paved the way for the punjabi nationalism as well as brought peace among Hindus and Muslims. In the north the sect was basically Vaisnava-based, but in its place of being focused on Visnu, it chose to focus itself on Vishnu's human incarnations, Rama and Krisna, the respective avatars or deities central to the two epics Ramayana and Mahabharata. For bhakti now Visnu's manifestations -Rama and Krishna- were the direct substance of devotion. Adoration of the devotees was focused on them relating with their respective companions: Sita with Rama; and Rukmini, his marital wife, or Radha, his Gopika companion, with Krishna. Images of these deities and their consorts set up in temples where worshipped. Fowler opines that the pathway of bhakti was not directly reachable to the lower castes; for them the path of prapatti – unquestioned self-surrender – was given. Singing of Bhajans and dancing created an important part of this adoration. The dancers were female slaves of the deity within the temple, but nagar-badhus outside. Apart from being tremendously ritualistic, the worship likely to be deeply emotional.

Followers of Bhakti movement in 12th and 13th Century included the saints such as Bhagat Namdev, and Saint Kabir Das who insisted on the devotional singing of praises of God through their own compositions. As the Bhakti movement was started before Guru Nanak, many historians have implied that Sikhism as started by Guru Nanak was nothing more than a Bhakti movement of Punjab. This is wrong in Toto and is in opposition to the basic Sikh virtues of equality of human beings and worship of single God. There is no doubt that Sikh Gurus accepted the singing of devotional songs in praise of lord from Bhakti but there is a huge difference between Bhakti, sufiism and Sikhism. Although Sufi and Bhakti saints are valued and recognized by Guru Granth Sahib but they do not form the main basis of Sikhism. Sikhism highlights on equality of male and female, good work ethic and as well as leading a good moral married life, which is Maya according to many Bhakti and sufi saints. Therefore, although Sikhs revere saints such as Bhagat Namdev, Bhagat Kabir and Sheikh Farid, but the ultimate Guru of a Sikh is the Guru Granth Sahib which includes about ten percent of the verses of these Saints.

Female poet-saints also played a major role in the Bhakti Movement in general. However, many of these women had to struggle for acceptance within the largely patriarchal movement. Only through demonstrations of their absolute devotion to the Divine, their marvelous poetry, and immovable insistence of their spiritual equality with their contemporaries were these women unwillingly accepted within their ranks. Their struggle attests to the strength of patriarchal values within both society and within religious and social movements attempting to pave the way for more democratic entrée to the Divine. The descriptions of Bhakti poetry is grounded in the everyday, recognizable language of ordinary people. Female bhaktas wrote of the obstacles of home, family bothering, the absent husband, meaningless household chores, and limits of married life, including their status as married women. In many cases, they rejected traditional women's roles and societal norms by leaving husbands and homes in total, choosing to become nomadic bhaktas; in some instances they formed communities with other saint-poets. Their new focus was utter devotion and worship of their Divine Husbands. While it is attractive to see women's participation within the Bhakti movement as a rebellion against the patriarchal norms of the time, there is little proof to support this perspective. Injustices and the patriarchal order itself were not a chief focus of these poet-saints. Women bhaktas were simply individuals trying to lead lives of devotion. Staying largely within the man dominated ideology that upheld the pure and dutiful wife as ideal, these women transferred the object of their devotion and their duties as the 'lovers' or 'wives' to their Divine or Husband. Nevertheless, their poetry became an integral aspect of the Bhakti movement at large is highly noteworthy and inspirational for many who look to these strange women as ideal examples of lives under the influence by love for the Divine.

Further, it would appear that with the movement's northward advancement its radical edge as it pertained to women's inclusion was tempered. Greater numbers of women took part in the movement's earlier progress -sixth to thirteenth centuries; it is largely male bhaktas and saints that are today perceived as the spokespersons for the movement in its later manifestations. The poetry of women bhaktas from this final time period is generally not indicative of a refusal of societal norms in terms of leaving family and homes in chase of divine love. Instead, some of the later poet-saints stayed within the confines of the household while clarifying on their souls' journeys, their eternal love for the God, as well as their continuing search for truth.

POPULAR LITERATURE

Popular literature includes those writings planned for the masses and those that find favors with bulky audiences. It can be different from artistic literature in the sense that it is designed mainly to entertain. Unlike high literature, popular literature generally doesn't seek a high degree of formal beauty or delicacy and is not proposed to endure. The development of popular literature has paralleled the spread of literacy through education and has been facilitated by scientific developments in printing. With the Industrial Revolution, works of literature, which were previously produced for using up by small, learned elites, became available to large sections and even the most of the members of a population. The border line between artistic and popular literature is misty, with much traffic between the two categories as current public preference and later critical assessment. While he was alive Shakespeare could be thought of as an author of popular literature, but now, he is regarded as a creator of artistic literature. Certainly, the main method of defining a work as belonging to popular literature is whether it is ephemeral, that is, losing its demand and importance with the passage of time. The most significant genre in popular literature is and forever has been the romance, extending as it does from the medieval ages to the present. The most common type of romance describes the obstacles encountered by two people -usually young-busy in a forbidden love. Another common genre is that of fantasy, or science fiction. Novels set in the western frontier of the U. S. in the nineteenth century, and called westerns, are also popular. Finally, the detective story or murder mystery is a broadly read kind of popular literature. Popular literature has also come to contain such genres as comic books and cartoon strips. There were the days when Indian writing in English was termed derivative and initiative: it has achieved free identity today. From Tagore to Naipaul, Indian English has gained international recognition. Because of colonization, followed by the English education at schools and colleges, English fiction is on the increase both in terms of readers and writers. Today, when our cities get hold of the Westernized trends, readers especially the youth, find it easier to join themselves to English novels than the novels in mother language.

A study of the Indian popular literature in English is a study of the expectations and trends of the masses which makes the study appropriate. The local and international events leave a trace in an average lifestyle of Indians which in turn will be reflected in his tastes. It is also psychoanalysis of the cultural standard of the society. English writers were present in India from the pre-independence epoch. V. S. Naipaul, Mulk Raj Anand, R. K. Narayan presented the Indian lifestyles to the world wide interest. As time passed, the female writers Anita Desai, Kamala Markhandaya and Shashi Deshpande created their space in national and international literature. Indian writers like Arundhati Roy and Aravind Adiga have won the impressive Man Booker Prize also. But, from the past two decades, Indian writing in English seems to pull masses more. The reason is that English narrative seems to be able to satisfy the expectations of people than other languages. English is read and enjoyed by people all over India so it gives a wider range of audience.

THE EMERGING TRENDS IN POPULAR FICTION

I. THE WESTERNIZATION IN CHARACTERIZATION AND STYLES

The trend to mimic the western popular fiction style is particularly noticeable. Today we have Ravi Subramanian, a banker, who writes thrillers associated to banking industry which is found very interesting by his viewers. His works include *I Boug ht a Monk's Ferrari , If God was a Banker and The Bankster* . He parallels himself to John Grisham, another popular writer of legal thrillers. Indian literature formerly regarded as a post-colonial literature has now completely morphed into the European standards. The Indian novels are not vivid any more. The pace is fast. The style is like to that of pulse-racing thrillers. An example, for the change of style is Vikas Swarup's *Q & A.Q & A* was the story of a boy from slums who takes part in a Television reality show and wins many rupees. The style is that of a thriller movie where the situation and visuals change fast keeping alive the suspense and adventure. It does not pictorise the heart breaking poverty of Indian downtrodden but rather follows a roller- coaster ride of thrills. The recent bestseller *Once upon the Tracks of*

Mumbai written by Rishi Vohra deals with the parallel theme in the psychotic and schizophrenic style. But India has not accepted the western outlook as a whole. In Europe, America and Africa, the autobiographical writings of gays, lesbians and middle sexes are very popular. In India such a trend has not yet been set. In novels which have a setting in metros, homosexuals come as secondary characters, but the readers have not grown so

broad minded enough to accept their life. The subject has become a hot topic for discuss in cities but when it comes to morality, Indians still consider this as a sinful act and an evil trait of Westernization.

THE FEMINIST WRITINGS

India has produced a number of female writers writing in English. Kamala Markhandaya, Shashi Deshpande, Anita Desai, Kiran Desai are among the long list. With the passage of time, the attitude of the society towards female writing is also undergoing a turbulent change. But not many Indian women writers have made it to bestsellers just. Kamala Markandaya's *Nectar in a Sieve* became a bestseller. Anita Desai's *Village by the Sea, In Custody and Cry, The Peacock* were once popular. But, these books became popular only abroad. However, Markandaya's *Bombay Tiger* (2008) and Anita Desai's *Zigzag Way* (2004) did not receive the same reaction as their earlier books did. Feminist attitude is strong but it doesn't address the real gender issues like family violence, female infanticide, contradiction in education to women, sexual abuses of women etcetera. This was more pronounced in writings in nineteen eighties and nineties. However, we cannot come into the conclusion that Indian readers are against to feminist writings. Shobha De's columns in *Outlook, The Times of India, and Stardust* are very popular amongst Indians. They might not have made it to the bestsellers but still her works are considered both feminist and popular. Her works like *Starry Lights (1989*) and *Socialite Evenings* (1989) depict stories of starlets, bright city lives, aspiration and love lives. The spicy style is obviously tempting to Indians. Meenaxi Reddy Madhavan's blogs were sensational in all over India. It was not just because of her innovative ideas but because of her playful and erotic content. She wrote under the pen name. Whenever a woman writes about love, sex and marital lives the people sense that it has an autobiographical element which makes the sales even better but certainly affects the author's confidentiality. Another female writer who was preyed by such bias and social banned was Kamala Das. The female characters in male writers' writings are also undergoing a change. Females are not any more the homemakers but multitasking motherly figures who manage the home affairs and office jobs. She has got attitude, career and an self-governing personality. In Chetan Bhagat's novel *Two States*, we can see the hero staying with his lover's family trying to impress her family. So the general societal attitude towards women are changing and it is honestly depicted the Indian popular fiction of both male and female writers.

THE I. I. T. WAY

The technocrats and managers seem to strike a daring for recent audience. The insider accounts of IITs and IIMs have become ultimate sellouts. The first writer to start this fashion was Chetan Bhagat, a pass out of IIT Delhi and IIM Ahmadabad. But later Sidin Vadakut's *Dork's series*, Neeraj Chibba's *Zero Percentile* also followed the style. It obviously shows the Indian preference for technocrats and professional jobs. The hi- fi job's glamour pulls people other than teaching, science research etcetera. Before a few decades Indian narratives used to cope with actors, strugglers, teachers and government workers. But today, the characters are new generation employees of Bank, call centre, internet café workers, copywriters etc. Such professions have come into fashion only from past 2 decades. The readers of English novels also include the city youth who wish for for such professions. So, obviously the competition in professional fields, the tight work schedules, the target completing rushes, placement worry etc. seem to take the attention of the audience.

TO EVIL HERITAGE PRACTISES

Indian writers in English have shown the honest picture of Indian domestics. Issues like, casteism, dowry, female infanticides et cetera were portrayed purposely Dalit writers like Dilp Chitre, Narayan Mane, Sharankumar Limbale were alarming to the marginalized culture. Dalit issues were highly sensitized by Indian writers writing in English. Mulk Raj Anand's *Untouchable*, *Coolie* etc. R. K. Narayan's *English Teacher* and *Dark Room* responded against the harmful practices in Indian marriages. Yet, today not many English writers turn their focus to public issues. An exception is Aravind Adiga's *The White Tiger (2008*) which was based on casteism and its aftermath. But the number of several social issues of India remains unexplored.

THE INDIANNESS OF INDIAN FICTIONAL CHARACTERS

Raja Rao stressed the Indianess of Indian writing in English. He highlighted the necessity of using the Indian English. The Gandhian philosophies and patriotic and local feelings were intentionally defended in his works. In the novel *Kanthapura,* we can see the characters addressing in local tongue and even the language giving highest justice to the translation of the

local tongue. The characters were Indians in feelings and deeds. Writers who write about villages and the stories which may be useless to the cities like David Davidar are appreciated in newspapers and also abroad. But today, his works are not found in bestseller lists. But, the characters may be Indians, but we cannot feel an Indian language's touch in their language. Amma, Appa, Papa, Maa is replaced by Mum, Dad etcetera. Even the conscience dialogues make it feels that the thought process is also in English. The conversational terminologies are similar to that of American fictions. It is, in a sense, an honest picture because the lifestyles are shifting towards Western World in metro cities especially. We cannot declare that the Indianess of writers is lost. However, the characters are becoming less Indian. The reason is that, the readers are more exposed to the Western lifestyles. To adjusted with their styles the characters also become pro- Westerners.

FROM VILLAGES TO METROS

Be it films or dramas or music, Indian art forms are shifting more towards small town and big cities. The villages make up more than half of the Indian population. Yet the readers seem to like the city life episodes. Therefore, the novel setting shifts from the villages to the towns. Mumbai, Delhi metros and abroad are the areas where major stories take place.

INFLUENCE OF INDIAN MYTHS

The Indian myths and epics still seem to encourage the audience but may be in a different package. Amit Tripathi's *The Secret of Naga (2012)* and Immortals of Meluha (2010) and Shashi Tharoor 's *The Great Indian Novel (1989)* are bestsellers that can be considered as exemplar. Tripathi gives a new direction to Lord Shiva's story in both his novels while Great Indian novel is presented in traditional Indian Epic Style of the Mahabharata and the Ramayana. Another bestseller, Ashwin Sanghi's *Chanakya's Chant* published in 2011 narrates the story of Chanakya and the scenery is Patna in 340 B.C. So it can be seen that Indian readership is still interested in epics, puranas, Indian history and myths.

ADAPTABILITY TO MOVIES

Today's Indian novels written in English are more frequently modified into movies. The reason is the changing narration style. The narration style of today's popular novels brings visuals to our brain. The fast pace, thriller style, the cinematic techniques of montage, quickly changing visuals help in edition. The thought process of people shift to visuals than words owing to impact of movies. It may be for this reason that this pattern shifts to narration. The descriptive form traditional style of postcolonial works is long lost. Anita Desai's *Zigzag* Ways was criticized for having descriptive styles, slow pace and less engaging characters. The authors also adapt their styles to viewers who watch movies. The modern Indian novels use more cinematic techniques and that's why can be easily adapted into movies. *Q & A, One Night at a Call Centre, Three Mistakes of my Life and 2 States verify* this. The pace of narration is also fast and pulse racing like a thriller. *One Night at a Call Centre* was adapted into a Bollywood film '*Hello*'; Three Mistakes of my Life was adapted into a movie '*Kai Po Che*'.

PERSISTING ORTHODOX MENTALITY

Salman Rushdie's *Satanic Verses* became a controversial book and it annoyed many protests and fatwas in India and abroad. A similar luck was faced *by* many writers like *Ram Swarup. The* attitude might have changed a bit but still Indian audience is very sensitive to the religious sentiments. Aravind Adiga's *White Tiger*, published in 2005, also caused debate. It can be concluded that though ages have passed, Indians are still very traditional in religious matters.

DIASPORA WRITING

Indian Diaspora always played an important part in Indian English literature. V. S. Naipaul, Salman Rushdie, Amitav Ghosh, Vikram Seth are prominent names among them. Amitav Ghosh's *River of Smoke* (2010) became a bestseller. Salman Rushdie's works are also popular in India. Aatish Thaseer, a British Indian journalist, is another Indian diaspora writer whose novels - *Noon (2011) and Temple-Goers (2010)* whose works have become popular in India. But the Diaspora's sense has to be widened. David Davidar's *House of Blue Mangoes*, *Ithaca* gained international attention but could not make its presence among Indian bestsellers. All his novels have the traditional storylines of villages and the style is also descriptive. The major reason is that the theme is Modern writers like Chetan Bhagat, Rishi Vohra and Aravind Adiga were employed and sometimes educated abroad. Their major works have been written while they were abroad. Therefore, the perspective might have a foreigner's ideas. The exposure to another country and their lifestyles can add to their experience as influence their novels. The perspective of looking at India becomes mixed with their exposure to the Indians abroad too and hence has a Diaspora trait.

The Existence and Significance of Genre

Perhaps the main debate adjoining popular fiction is the significance and meaning of genre. Literary generic categories, as we understand them in the United States, have existed since the nineteen thirties, although dedicated scholarly attention began only in the nineteen seventies. Frederic Jameson's article *Magical Narratives: Romance as Genre* argued that 'genres are essentially contracts between a writer and his readers; or rather … they are literary institutions … like other agreements or contacts'.

This declaration of the nature of literary genre was an addition to a widespread theoretical debate that dates back to Aristotle's Poetics. In recent decades the finer points of genre and generic difference have become an increasingly bulky issue in some academic fields, engaged by writers as different like Northrop Frye, Frederic Jameson, Tzvetan Todorov, Jacques Derrida, and Carolyn Miller. The use of genre as a method of social analysis has expanded to contain the field of communications, for instance, and is now applied in the form of speech action to subjects such as Presidential addresses—in this view; almost every act of communication belongs to a certain genre. These hypothetical debates could be easily applied to the study of popular literature, but are often fully ignored or not overtly referenced. Jameson's insight into the close connection between readers and writers predated Radway's ethnographic work, but its ripples took almost a decade to hit the shoreline. Often citing Jameson, critics since the late nineteen eighties have understood genres as relational and historical categories that change over time in response to political and social conditions, such as technological developments, corporate ownership, publishing, and the random tastes of readers themselves. Some have questioned how genres have been formed and represented by the canonization of specific works, an argument which echoed the canon-making debates in schools and universities in the United States in the nineteen eighties. Writers such as Kathleen Gregory Klein have claimed that since canonical authors are generally male, conservative critics have misunderstood whole genres through their biased choices of representative texts. In reply to these challenges to the critical application of the concept of genre, many scholars have reasserted its implication. Their claims are worth noting. First, readers often strengthen generic walls by devoting themselves to one genre to the omission of all others. Second, genres, especially established categories such as crime literature, are often self-referential:

texts refer and respond to the genre's traditions, a game within a game that fans expect and enjoy. Third, the existence of generic partition is reified by material factors: for instance, the blurbs on the back of novels -almost always provided by authors from the same genre-, the genre's name printed on each book, and the categorization of popular fiction in the physical organization of most bookstores. *The Direction of the Generic Approach* Putting aside, for the moment, the question of the value of a genre based move toward the popular fiction studies, the literary genres that most critics identify—the thriller, Western, romance, fantasy, etc.—were categorized and calcified over 5 decades ago and should be altered in general. Genres do remain important to readers, but as Derek Longhurst points, they continually evolve in reaction and relation to the world. Although marginal writers such as Walter Mosely have begun to appropriate major genres along the feminist model, minority characters should not have to appear in conventional genres to value scholarly attention, as they often have. Particularly African-American genres, for instance, have existed for at least four decades but have been almost entirely overlooked by academics. 'Gangsta' fiction of the nineteen seventies, with its focus on pimps and street revolutionaries, has had a major following and political influence. Other than the popular Iceberg Slim, Donald Goines has sold more books than any other African- American author in history. Today's street fiction, written and overcame by black medieval women, among others, offers amazing tales of tough love by prolific authors such as Zane and Noire and is sold in droves on the Internet and on street corners in major cities. Both genres are almost entirely disregarded by scholars.

A number of minor genres, not as popular as thrillers and romances but nevertheless possessing formulas and 'contracts' with devoted readers, are similarly under the critical radar. For instance, the collection *Political Mythology and Popular Fiction,* written fully by political scientists, identifies 'middle-class fiction', the historical novel, the small-town American novel, the sports novel, and America-at-war fiction. Such a shift would require an even greater alertness of readers, but the study of reception has undergone a great deal of recent appreciation. First, critics say, reception often reduces a complex solid network of cultural practices and relationships to interpretations that depend on one or two determining factors like race or gender. Second, the question of supremacy and resistance, scholars tend to romanticize readers' responses as proof of independent creativity or resistance. Third, audience research makes falsely trustworthy claims and is also often treated as a scientific 'slice of reality.' Because researchers' certainty bring biases to their work, attempts to uncover readers' understandings and conceptions of individual texts amount to second-order interpretation. These arguments are convincing, but they should be regarded as cautionary reminders. One might call forth once again the words of Stephen Knight, who admitted that although his Form and Ideology in Crime Fiction would be more influential with more attention to readership,

> It has seemed better to make a beginning, to offer analysis, than to remain silent about audiences as most literary criticism does[20]. (Knight :1980,78)

Although a methodological overemphasis on reception can be illusory, studies such as Reading the Romance show that attention to reception—even if it is technically impossible to arrive at an unbiased representation, and even if it must be irritated by an acknowledgement of the limits of the chosen method— is necessary in a field that is so obviously reliant on its readers for its shape and direction. An instructive example is the field of American history, where the rise of social and cultural history in the nineteen seventies has challenged the value of the objectivity question. If 'objectivity' is agreed to be an impractical mean, critics should adjust their prospect and allow mixed, interdisciplinary methodologies to respond to a new series of questions.

6

Coffee Table Books in Popular Culture

A coffee table book is a hardcover book that is planned to sit on a coffee table or equivalent surface in an area where guests sit and are entertained, thus inspiring conversation or improving monotony. They tend to be oversized and of heavy construction, since there is no pressing need for portability. Subject matter is generally confined to non-fiction, and is usually visually dominated. Pages consist mainly of photographs and illustrations, accompanied by captions and small blocks of text, as opposite to long prose. Since they are premeditated at anyone who might pick the book up for a light read, the analysis inside is often more basic and with less jargon than other books on the subject. Because of this, the term *coffee table book* can be usfed pejoratively to indicate a shallow approach to the subject.

History

David R. Brower is sometimes credited with inventing the modern coffee table book.[21] (*http://www.sierraclub.org/educationleconte/wood_hr2715_11-15-03.asp*) While serving as supervisory director of the Sierra Club, he had the idea for a series of books that combined nature cinematography and writings on nature, with, as he put it, a page size big enough to carry a given image's vibrant. The eye must be required to move about within the boundaries of the image, not cover it all in one glance. The first such book, *This is the American Earth*, with photographs by Ansel Adams and others and text by Nancy Newhall, published in 1960;

> The series became known as the "Exhibit Format" series, with 20 titles eventually published. [22] (Natiral Vision)

The concept of a book intended essentially for display over perusal was mentioned much earlier by Michel de Montaigne in his essay *Upon Some Verses of Virgil,*

> I am vexed that my Essays only serve the ladies for a common movable, a book to lay in the parlor window...[23] (Montaigne: 1580, 122)

Almost two centuries later, Laurence Sterne in his comic novel *The Life and Opinions of Tristram Shandy,* Gentleman advanced the more cheerful vision that As his life and opinions are likely to make some noise in the world, and be no less read than the Pilgrim's Progress itself- and, in the end, prove the very thing Montaigne dreaded his Essays should turn out, that is, a book for a parlor window.

In popular culture

Coffee table books have been featured in many areas of popular culture. In the nineteen eighties, British comedy duo Smith and Jones released the lavishly-tooled Smith and Jones Coffee Table Book — its cover was designed to look as if the book could dual as a coffee table. The fifth season of the sitcom Seinfeld included a story arc involving Kramer wanting to write a coffee table book about coffee tables. His idea was for the coffee table book to have legs built into the back cover and coasters built into the face cover, so the book itself could be turned into a small coffee table. In the Family Guy episode *You Can't Do That on Television, Peter*. Peter states that he, Joe Swanson and Glen Quagmire are making a coffee table book of lesbian butts in nineteen eighties denims. Late-night talk show Conan features a sketch called Coffee Table Books That Didn't Sell, in which Conan O'Brien reviews several –fake- coffee table books with unusual and ridiculous premises, such as Animals on Meth or Movie Stars With Their Eyes Pushed Closer Together.

7

Popular Fiction Studies: The Advantage of a New Field

Stephen Knight's Form and Ideology in Crime Fiction, begins with the claim that not very much has been written about crime fiction. This was true in relative terms; even if a great deal had, really, been written about crime fiction, the most celebrated and conservatively literary of popular forms, it was only a stream compared to the flood of work that flourished in the nineteen eighties. Crime fiction and other established genres of popular novels—such as romance, thriller, science fiction, horror novel and Western—have each drawn extensive attention from a variety of disciplinary and methodological perspectives, but they have more often than not been considered and analyzed as unequal categories. 'Popular fiction' as a general object of study has hardly ever been explored, in part because it is often included under the sunshade of popular culture. This is a mistake; just as film and television have developed their own app roaches that reflect the unique social, cultural, political, and industrial dimensions of each medium, so popular fiction should inhabit its own critical space. 'Popular fiction' has been defined in a number of ways -in Western, English-language criticism- over the last half-century.

Although the specific terminology has often echoed the writer's approach to the topic, Matthew Schneider-Mayerson *Studies in Popular Culture* the subject's actual domain is rarely questioned. Popular fiction is defined by what it is not literature. Most critics openly or totally stick to the following claims: Whereas literature is indifferent to the marketplace, original, and complex, popular fiction is simple, affective, overstated, exciting, and mechanical 'Real' writers spend decades worrying over each sentence, while genre hacks produce a new paperback each year, to be 'consumed' in airports and quickly discarded. A persistent thorn in definitions of popular culture is the vagueness of the word 'popular'. If a literary novel—by Philip Roth, for instance—sells more copies than Nora Roberts latest romance, *which is "popular"? Can both be? Is the definition qualitative or quantitative?* The importance of this distinction was highlighted by the argument surrounding Jonathan Franzen's *rejection of Oprah* Winfrey's official endorsement of his novel *The Corrections*. When Franzen said in 2001, -I see this as my book, my creation, and I didn't want that logo of corporate ownership on it,- he publicly eluded the wall between real literature and popular fiction, a distinction which would exist no matter how many copies *The Corrections* might sell. The contrast amid popular fiction and literature occurs against the backdrop of ongoing debates about the categories low and high culture by authors such as Lawrence Levine and Andreas Huyssen, but the study of popular fiction requires its own attention. Although many of the aforesaid terms used to stereotype popular fiction have been questioned by scholars, most would agree on a basic distinction: a novel is popular fiction if its success is measured -by the public and its publisher- as much by its sales and the devotion of fans as different to timeless literary quality.

A Brief History of Popular Fiction Criticism

In the nineteen sixties, American scholars showed little interest in popular fiction, and when they mentioned the subject, primarily in English departments, it was, as sociologist Tony Bennett put it, primarily to present popular fiction as evidence of "Both symptom and cause of a generalized social problem of cultural degeneracy." [24] (Bennett: 1990, 11)

Early works viewed genres a historically and simply applied conventional methodology of literary criticism to more wide-read fiction. Two chief examples are Bruce Merry's *Anatomy of a Spy Thriller* and Jerry Palmer's *Thrillers: Genesis and Structure of a Popular Genre.* Both are extremely indebted to Northrop Frye's *Anatomy of Criticism,* focus wholly on the written texts themselves, as opposed to, for example, their political economy or reception, and presume a simple relationship of straight influence between readers and the novels. Although both studies yield insights into the thriller—Merry sees it in the context of the Cold War, while Palmer focuses on competitive masculine individualism and conspiratorial fears in the U. S.—their assertions about what the genre means are based almost totally on their presumed status as literary experts. A shocking amount of criticism still follows this model. One often-cited example is Walter Nash's *Language in Popular Fiction*, in 1990. Nash, originally a medievalist, has written on subjects ranging from comedy to rhetoric but is perhaps best known for Language in Popular Fiction. *Language* mirrored the lasting popularity of New Criticism; concerned primarily with women's magazines and action fiction, Nash ignores new developments in literary criticism, such as the significance of ideology, structuralism and historicism. In its place, he provides a sheer reading of the language of a variety of novels, from which he draws conclusions about their genres. Given the enormous amount of popular fiction made available in each genre every year, his selection is not nearly large enough to maintain his confident generalizations. More notably, though Nash's focus on style certainly contributes to the study of popular fiction, his lack of attention to social and political background, readership, and political economy limits the potential of his work.

New Perspectives in the 1980s

The profusion of book-length studies of popular culture published in the nineteen eighties was the result of the influence of feminine world, the New Left, and, within the academy, cultural studies, but it should also be recognized as a reaction to the myopia of New Criticism. One of the first cracks in the dam was the English translation of Pierre Macherey's *A Theory of Literary Production*, which applied an Althusserian 'symptomatic' reading to Matthew Schneider- Mayerson *Studies in Popular Culture* literary texts, specifically the works of Jules Verne. Macherey's work, deeply dependent on psychoanalytic criticism, broke new ground in its attempt to see popular fiction as reflective of sociopolitical currents, whereas previous critics simply considered social context as background or mirror on writer's biography. Besides, Macherey fundamentally challenged earlier criticism by exposing and denouncing the 'interpretive fallacy' of many critics—that their task was to discover and explain the singular meaning contained in a certain text. This simple acknowledgement delegitimized expert readings and opened the way to severe studies of reader's response. Macherey's work, along with a general shadowing of the lines between high and low culture that we now connect with postmodernism, were powerful influences on Janice Radway's ingenious study of romance readers, *Reading the Romance: Women, Patriarchy, and Popular Literature* published in nineteen eighty four. In re-introduction to the work, often considered the best study of popular fiction to date, Radway traced its intellectual genesis to a debate within American Studies, which at that point still tended to suppose that the history and 'character' of the United States could be incidental from its classic literature. She not only focused on *popular* literature but asserted that

> If literature is to be treated as a document in the study of culture, it is first necessary to know something about who reads, why they do so, and how they go about it. [25] (Radway: 1994, 9)

Radway's study was a charming combination of approaches; a loose ethnography of viewers that represented an unusual attention to reception of literature and a detailed history of the political economy of publishing, with feminist psychoanalysis at its interpretive center.

Each of these strains was reflected in later criticism. Radway's broadest involvement was her attention to social context, which was influenced by the turn towards social history within history departments. Although Radway was unacquainted of the developments happening in the field that has come to be known as cultural studies, mainly at the Centre for Contemporary Cultural Studies at the University of Birmingham, they paralleled major aspects of her approach and were similarly principal. Following the model of Thompson, Richard Hoggart, Althusser and above all Antonio Gramsci, authors such as Stuart Hall, Dick Hebdige and John Storey credited popular culture with political and aesthetic significance. The first fruits of this line of thought in the study of popular fiction were two studies published by Michael Denning in 1987, *Mechanic Accents* in particular was a beautiful combination of literary study, archival research, and social history that has much in common with *Reading the Romance*: a focus on the political economy of literary production that structured a detailed examination of readers; a special awareness of the role of one category of identity, gender in Radway's case and class in Denning's; and a clever respect of the way that popular books constitute a contested landscape, a field of cultural clash where signs with wide appeal and tone take on contradictory costumes and are spoken in contrary actions. If prior critics of popular fiction might be seen as endorsing the 'culture industry' perspective put forth by Adorno and Horkheimer, Radway and Denning replace top-down meaning-making with a hegemonic field where reception is as essential as production.

Attention to reception in one form or another became the norm for studies of popular fiction in the nineteen eighties. This echoed a turn towards reception of media audiences in general, in part as a result of David Morley's *The 'Nationwide' Audience,* which pioneered a critical approach in which watching television was considered a complex cultural practice. The general effect of similar ethnographic and social turns in other disciplines, such as literary studies, communication, and history, was similarly extraordinary. Although the pendulum of stress and methodology has not swung all the way towards readers, there has been a distinct turn towards reception as a potentially transgressive act since the nineteen eighties, especially amongst feminist critics. If there has been one dominant influence on the study and writing of popular novels over the last 25years, it has been the activist intellectual work of feminism.

The Feminist Influence

Especially in the nineteen eighties, many feminist scholars were drawn to popular fiction via the popularity of romance novels. Feminism, an activist movement whose academic representatives often maintain a strong connection to the 'real' world, has led to methodologies and epistemologies that support the study of popular over selected texts. The first noteworthy publication was Germaine Greer's polemic *The Female Eunuch*, which argued that romance novels soothed, deceived, and manipulated their womanly readers and should be shunned by women. Radway's study was motivated in part by this hasty reaction to romance novels, as was Tania Modleski's similarly sophisticated and fair *Loving With a Vengeance: Mass-Produced Fantasies for Women.*

Representative of general feminine interest in the romance was the collection *The Progress of the Romance: The Politics of Popular Romance* (1986), which generally supported the work of Radway and Modleski, rejecting the assumption that readers were passive imbibers of patriarchal propaganda. This work, often termed 'appropriation' because of its deliberate effort to reclaim popular fiction from those who see only control by both traditional literary critics and the 'culture industry', was at first rarely applied to other genres of popular literature. Early efforts, in the late nineteen seventies, were modest in ambition: feminists searched for strong female characters, veiled critique of hierarchy, or a validation of difference and community in crime novels.

In the last 2 decades, feminist scholars such as Priscilla L. Walton, Manina Jones, and Merja Makinen have begun to reinterpret other genres, especially crime and detective novels, while feminist *authors* write clearly feminist popular fiction of all stripes. In addition to questioning the formation of patriarchal canons and more readily acknowledging and studying rising genres, many female critics have followed Radway's replica of moving critical interpretation towards reader reception.

Popular Fiction as a Field

The prospect of the study of popular fiction is difficult to guess. We have seen the two leading modes. The first is the traditional, text-oriented, formulaic approach that sees popular fiction as a meretricious cousin of actual literature. The second is the feminist-cultural studies approach, which views in readers the ability and propensity to reinterpret texts that are seemingly traditional and patriarchal in a resistant, transgressive, unpredictable and socio-politically informed manner. On the other hand, a number of recent developments suggest that new and often more complicated approaches are on the scope, often occasioned by criticisms of the apparent rigid binary of these two modes. The term popular fiction—as compared to literature—itself manifests the dissimilarity between these two approaches, along with the distinction between authors such as Nora Roberts and Franzen. In this way, renaming the field 'popular literature' might signal a third way to these critical boundaries. The issue of genre itself remains at the heart of almost every general study of popular fiction. Apart from three exceptions, notably Jerry Palmer's *Potboilers: Methods, Concepts and Case Studies in Popular Fiction,* McCracken's *Pulp: Reading Popular Fiction*, and Gelder's *Popular Fiction: The Logics and Practices of a Literary Field*, all principally connected with British literature, there has been little attempt to fuse the field of popular fiction despite the obvious continuities between different genres. Critics, publishers, and readers are all put in in the continued existence of generic limitations for very different grounds, but there are a number of convincing arguments to move beyond genre in future learning. First, as noted above, the reality of generic categories tends to lead scholars toward single-dimensional conceptualizations. For romance readers, it is their status as women; for Denning's dime novels readers, their position as the working-class. At last, the existence of bestsellers looks to challenge the importance of genre. Bestsellers tend to cross generic borders, either engaging two or more genres or mixing the formulas of both. In her *The Readers' Advisory Guide to Genre Fiction published in* 2001, Joyce J. Jaricks attempts to help librarians speechless by reader requests by creating a list of 'sure bets' that almost all readers will enjoy. What do bestsellers and sure bets tell us about the relevance of the concept of genre and existing genres? What do they unveil about genre readers? The conventional imagination of genre readers, created by ethnographies such as *Reading the Romance*, depicts fans of popular fiction as individuals or groups devoted to their literary position, often devouring page-turners at an impressive clip. But if the average reader is in fact a traveler selecting up a novel with a noticeable cover at an airport, should genres remain the central axis of analysis? This is a question that Jameson phrased nearly two decades back. In an article, *Towards a New Awareness of Genre published in 1984*, he argues that in lieu of placing a novel in a genre as if we were dropping it into a bucket, we might triangulate works *among* different genres. If a book was concurrently a Western and street fiction, how does this alter the neat formulas of literary critics? Perhaps most importantly, how might this new perspective mirror the social, cultural, and political context in which it was published and consumed? This would be one of the primary concerns of the field of popular fiction studies; a fresh approach to genre criticism and the significance of genre itself. Inside the study of popular culture, popular fiction is the semi developed brother of film and television studies. One advantage of considering popular fiction as a separate field would be to separate its particular political economy and cultural position. More awareness must be paid to the specific factors of consumption. For instance, publishers and booksellers can attest that book covers and a novel's placement in a bookstore—both the factors that are directly fused into the political economy of publishing—may be as important as content in determining sales. Greater attention to them would be a productive step toward understanding

consumer choices and the relationship between political and industrial factors- such as shifts in corporate ownership- and the success of individual books. Really, one further advantage of considering a subject as a 'field' is to form scholars who focus in it. Currently, the majority of authors who come up to the genres of popular fiction, and many of the most insightful, do so as an isolated project, an outlier in an academic career dedicated to other pursuits. One might expect that scholars working in an acknowledged field might be freer and academically interested in pursuing in greater deepness the approaches sketched here.

The study of popular fiction remains in its childhood, subject to expert interpretations and supposition by academics that may be quite out of touch with the regular reader. As other subjects are mined for new perspectives and further complications of leading narratives in a progressively more packed academy, the formation of the field of popular fiction presents a productive opportunity to extend a greater understanding of American popular culture.

CONCLUSION

Today, marketing of any product is very critical for success. Like all, in novels also marketing skill matters and this is particularly noticeable in Indian novels in English. At the closing stages of the day, sales will depend on how first-class the marketing was. This does not mean that the best sellers have poor creative content but it means that if marketing is not done well there might not be enough sales that a novel actually ought to have. Better marketing skills mean so much more audience for the work and hence the one with most marketing capacity becomes the bestsellers.

Today we can find a lot of technocrats, management professionals particularly from abroad making bestsellers in India. The credits can be given both to marketing skills and imaginative writing skills. The social networking media are also helping in marketing. Many writers like Chetan Bhagat, Shobha De, Anita Desai, Kiran Desai have Face book fan pages and they are also active in Twitter and Blog. This helps them to know more about the needs of the audience and helps in direct communication. Even books are accessible on e-reading. Many authors publish excerpts of their books online for encouraging sales. Today, the habit of reading is declining. So the writers have got to keep up more to the taste of audience and their skyrocketed life. The audience needs maximum amusement in smallest amount of time and effort. However, the Indian English popular fiction portrays the taste of Indian authors and therefore can be analyzed as a cultural study material.

Indian English literature and its historical development had happened together with the consolidation of British colonialism in the country. There however exists a variety of opinions about the first perfect Indian English text, although critics come to the agreement that history of Indian literature in English dates back to at least the early nineteenth century. Its beginnings had received their momentum from three sources, the first is, the British government's education transformation, second is, the attempt of missionaries and the third is, the response and acceptance of English literature and language by the Indian upper-class. The basic historical viewpoint of Indian English literature is an effort to contextualize the growth and rise of the genre from its beginning to its present day glory. First, there were the educational reformers called forth by both the charter Act of 1813 and the English Education Act 1835 of William Bentick. In an attempt to correct and equalize some of the materialistic and famished, therefore compromising, practices of the East India Company servants, the English parliament had shown the green signal to the Charter Act, which had made England accountable for the educational betterment of the natives. The subsequent English Education Act, encouraged by Thomas Babington Macaulay's *ill-famed minute on Indian education*, made English the medium of Indian education and English literature a penalizing subject in Indian educational institutions. and has natured from a seedling to a firmly rooted tree that blooms with its completely still awaiting its upcoming metamorphosis. Indians however, did not take to penning in English in a day it look umpteen historical events and memorable and remarkable personalities to bring Indian English Literature to its contemporary eminence. Indian literature in English though possesses a fairly recent history; it has actually got only one and half century maturity.

In The Beginning...

The first English writing by any Indian as it has been appeared so far is Sake Dean Mahomet's travelogue *Travels of Dean Mahomet*. This book was published in the year seventeen ninety three from England. Sake Dean Mahomet was an Indian warrior from Bihar in the British Armed Force and was carried to Britain by his chief Captain Godfrey Evan Baker after his retirement, seeing that Din Mohammad was a good cook. Dean later learnt English rationally and wrote down his notes in Britain. But it is outstanding Indian writing as the British colonial rulers were not paying attention in English education rather they were stressing importance to educate citizens in their native vernacular language. It was actually Raja Ram Mohan Ray and other social campaigners of that time who made the Britishers kick off English with vernaculars into the schools as a medium of learning.

Michael Madhusudan Dutt and Bankim Chandra Chatterjee were two well-known writers of that time who started writing in English. Dutt wrote epic verse in English while Chatterjee wrote his introductory novel *Rajmohan's Wife*. The novel was started in sequential form in a magazine from the year 1864 but didn't appear as a book until the year 1935. It is exciting to point that both Dutt and Chatterjee returned back to English writing again and they recognized themselves as well known personalities in native Bengali literature. Toru Dutt, one more instance of that time, was a very young teen age girl when she decorated her poems and novels in French and English languages. She died at the age of twenty two and at the time of her death, she left behind two unpublished novels— *Le Journal de Mademoiselle d'Arvers* --believed to be the first novel in French by an Indian writer-- and *Bianca,* or *the Young Spanish Maiden* --thought to be the first novel in English by an Indian woman writer. Besides, she had also written two shortened volumes of original poems in English titled as *Ancient Ballads and Legends of Hindustan.*

The Mid-Section...

English writing became more well-liked with the rise of Nationalism in the later period of the 19th century into the early period of 20th century. The English Language became a sharp and strong gazette with which one can express close feelings to British rulers. Dadabhai Navroji wrote *Poverty and Un--British Rule in India* in which he brought notice to the demanding of India's wealth into Britain and Surendra Nath Banerjee started to circulate an English newspaper called *The Bengali* by which he extend liberal ideas and patriotic messages to the citizens. Later, the freedom struggle resulted in an activist brand of writing by Bal Gangadhar Tilak, Lala Lajpat Ray, Mahatma Gandhi, Aurobindo Ghose, T. Prakasham, Kasturi Rnaga Iyer, and Sarojini Naidu. In addition to this, writing in their vernacular native languages, they also accepted the English language to express their emotion and anguish. These personalities not only expressed their ideas throughout critical essays but developed in other forms of literature too. Tagore sets up his Bengali poems to English readers by translation whereas Naidu's romanticism captivated English readers through her poems. Mahatma Gandhi's *An Experiment with Truth* and Jawaharlal Nehru's *Glimpses of Indian History* & *The Discovery of India* were all recognized as necklace of Indian writings in English. These writings were not written for the British readers at all. Rather, they were written for the Indian readers who felt comfortable with English because the English language is heterogeneous and had taken a position to be in touch with the different native languages and it was no more with any colonial characteristics. English thus became an Indian language and a fluent and easy media in which to express one's ideas to the world.

Later in the nineteen thirties, R.K. Narayan, Raja Rao and Mulk Raj Anand played a major role in English writing with their fiction. They three were considered as the 'basic poles of the Indian English novel'. Mulk Raj Anand's novel *Untouchable* published in the year 1935 proves itself as a leading of 'dalit writings' in Indian literature. It is the story of a single day in the life of Bakha, a toilet-cleaner, who by chance thrashed with a member of a higher caste. Famous amongst his novels are *The Village* published in the year 1939, *Across the Black Waters* (1940), *and The Sword and the Sickle* (1942), all were written in England, and *Coolie* (1945), and *The Private Life of an Indian Prince* (1953) which were in black and white in India. He was among the first authors to give Punjabi and Hindustani idioms into English. Raja Rao was considered a National novelist. His novel *Kanthapura* published in the year 1938 was an account of the impact of Gandhiji's preaching on peaceful struggle against the British. His other novel *The Serpent and the Rope* is a work performing the relationships between Indian and Western civilization. The serpent in the title refers to delusion and the cord to reality.

R.K. Narayan is one of the most famed and broadly read Indian novelists even in recent days too. He wrote plentiful novels like *Swami and Friends* published in the year 1935, *The Bachelor of Arts* (1937), *The Dark Room* (1938), *The English Teacher* published in the year 1944, *Mr. Sampath-The Printer of Malgudi* in the year 1949, *The Financial Expert* (1952), *The Vendor of Sweets* (1967), *The Painter of Signs* (1976), *A Tiger for Malgudi* (1983), *Talkative Man* (1986) and *The World Of Nagaraj* in 1990. Besides, he wrote a few short stories on the subject of Malgudi, a fictitious semi-urban town situated in southern India. He was awarded by Sahitya Academy for his novel *The Guide* published in the year 1958. In the year 1980, The Royal Society of Literature gave the A.C. Benson award to R.K. Narayan and was made an Honorary Member of the American Academy and Institute of Arts and Letters. His style is more vivid, less analytical, and rooted in a separate spirit, providing for a more genuine and realistic narration where he successfully employed the use of gradation dialogic prose with gentle Tamil overtones which is based on the nature of his characters.

In the post-colonial period, Indian Writing in English has changed its direction and a vast change has been observed in the characteristics. The 'societal subjects' have been lessened and an 'individual' has emerged in the writings. Kamala Markanday, Vikram Seth, Bharati Mukherjee, Salman Rushdie, Vikram Chandra, Gita Mehta, Anita Desai, Kiran Desai, Arundhati Roy, Chitra Banerjee Divakaruni, Raj Kamal Jha, Jhumpa Lahiri, Bharti Kirchner, Khushwant Singh, Tarun Tejpal, Amit Chaudhuri, Amitav Ghosh, Vikas Swarup, Rohinton Mistry, Vijay Singh, Suketu Mehta, Kiran Nagarkar, Dr. Birbal Jha ,and C.R. Krishnan have been some noteworthy writers of the post-colonial period who have made Indian Writing in English more well-liked in abroad than in India. Some of writers like Kamala Markanday, Salman Rushdie, Bharati Mukherjee, Anita Desai, Kiran Desai have moved themselves away from the country to abroad. Therefore, a question is raised as to whether their writings can be treated as genuine Indian writings?? Rajendra Yadav, a noted Hindi writer once complained that the Indian Writing in English take a haphazard look at India, like Pankaj Mishra›s work *The Romantics*, where he is simply a tourist who does not know the inner psyche of the people or the more clever mechanism Vikram Seth uses in a novel *A Suitable Boy*, the pretext of looking for a bridegroom, which takes him to different locales and professions. It is a creatively written traveler's guide. They travel into our culture portrays a bit of our geography; their total approach is to westerners: a third-rate serpent and a rope trick.

V.S. Naipaul, the Nobel Prize winner and one of India's Diaspora writers, once assumed that Indian English writers are responsible for making a body of literature in expel mainly written by writers and read by readers living outside the country. Altaf Tyrewala, the writer of the novel *No God In Sight*, also criticizes these NRIs, who place themselves as front liners in the eyes of Western readers and Western media and that these writers live in the First World and write on the subject of the Third, traveling for a month or so to India in order to collect material on which to base their writings. There were a few western writers starting from Rudyard Kipling to Mark Tully, Dominique Lapiere and William Dalrymple who have remained the chief time of their lives in India, wrote their texts on India and Indian people, but our critics never incorporated them with Indian Writing in English writers as their race was different. Writer of the novel *The Impressionist* and *Transmission,* Hari Kunzru, asked a severe question if we reject these types of writings as Indian writings, how and why we include the writings of Naipaul, Salman Rushdie, Vikram Seth, Hari Kunzru and the Desai as India writings, while the first group came to India and the second group moved away from India?? Kunzru asserts that he is not an Indian writer but a British one, thus categorically rejecting any claim that Indians might blame of him being an Indian Writing in English. The position of the outsider is of great importance to the fitness of any society. The worry is that in the last twenty years, India, typically for a globalizing country, has not hypothesized a position for the outsider or for the misfit or for collapse. Its rhetoric is concerned with success in various ways. In India, everybody is some way in some kind of nexus of power. We need to recapture that space for the irresponsible. And what better way to seek that subtle vantage point than to move away from the nexus and observe it with an unemotional eye.

Presently...

Today, writers from Russia, France, Italy, and even Latin America, anyway, write in English, but their writings are considered as magnum opus of universal writings. Their writings are copiously available through English version and have been attached a label as Russian writing or French writing or Italian writing, or Latin American writing. But when the question of Indian writing comes up, critics run for Rushdie or Vikram Seth, for getting that Indian writing has a long lasting tradition. At a reception prepared at Santiniketan to pay respect to Rabindranath Tagore's literary genius after he had been awarded by the Nobel Prize in Literature, Tagore believed that his insult and infamy that was a lot to suffer at the hands of the country were not negligible in quantity and so long he had tolerated them with internal stamina. In this context, he has not been able to understand obviously why he received honor from outside. He did not know that God, whom he had offered homage sitting on the Eastern shore, would extend his right arm in the western shore to believe the same. Europe has given him the velvet garland of honor. If it carries any value, it lies in the artistic sense of the men of culture of that country. That has no direct connection with our country. It can be understood easily, how our authentic Indian writings are being overlooked by us who placed in the chair to umpire what Indian writing is and what is not. Our misjudgment make both the actual writings unnoticed and also signify the mask as Indian Literature beneath which India remains invisible to global readers. When we read the works of Garcia, we could encounter Latin America, with all its essence, cultural milieu, lives and tradition. But in bestsellers, Indian Writing in English in western countries basically depicts the lives of Indian Diaspora and their unknown culture. Post-colonial literature cannot be planned by neglecting literary works in the original languages of nations. The post-colonial literature has been termed after getting many suggestions. Universal questions frequently asked are, what is the new cultural identity of the country after independence has been obtained? Who is really in power here? How and Why an independence day really means independence? And where does an individual fit in this frame of the country and how he or she makes a living? In fact, actual Indian post-colonial writings that are accessible with regional writings and English writings get, in some extent, separated from the people and country.

TheEnchantressofFlorence by SalmanRushdie, *Unaccustomed Earth* by Jhumpa Lahiri, *Sea of Poppies* by Amitav Ghosh, *Past Continuous* by Neel Mukherjee and *Escape* by Manjula Padmanabhan were selected for the Vodafone-Crossword Book Awards in 2008 and the award was given together to Amitav Ghosh and Neel Mukherjee. Ghosh had to share the award with Mukherjee because his introductory novel is the first attempt in Indian writing to explore exchange sexuality, though Vikram Seth has been diplomatic but not secretive about his views on gay and bisexual orientation, depicting this alternative sexuality in his novels *The Golden* Gate & *A Suitable Boy* in very unclear way. Similarly, Jhumpa Lahiri's effort to portray the complexity of one's identity concerning with one's name opens a new vistas for Indian literature through her novel *The Nameshake*. But these trends were prevelent in other Indian writings before than Seth or Lahiri or Mukherjee. From the nineteen fifties, one can distinguish a change in the style of Indian writing. The Indian writers became bolder and stronger in expressing their emotional wants. Marxism, Existentialism, Magic Realism and all modern trends of global literature are not safe and sound in Indian writings and in relationship to English writings; these Indian Literatures are not covering behind any more. Jagadish Mohanty is a major personality in Oriya Literature and is considered a leader in Oriya fiction. He has also been regarded as the prime figure in the introduction of 'existentialism' to Literature. His novel *Nija Nija Panipathwas,* published in 80s, where the protagonist, a Brahmin young boy from coastal Orissa, flies to the plateau region of Western Orissa and purchases a job card of a fake tribal name Samaru Khadia from a job provider mafia group and is employed at the firewood fields there. The protagonist begins to find everything regarding his individuality seems to be in disaster as he is not *he* but another person with a total diverse self. This novel was sequential and was published in book form much earlier than the publication of Lahiri's *The Name Shake.* It is only because Mohanty has not been translated that his praise had been limited to Oriya people only. Similarly in the year 1927, a Hindi writer, Pandey Bechan Sharma, better known by his fictitious name Ugra which means extreme, had published a book, and collection of ten short stories entitled *Chocolate.* These stories are on gay sexuality. The book provided a nationalist construction of Indian uniqueness, especially in relation to ideas of India's past, gender, masculinity and sexuality, and of Hindu-Muslim, and India-foreign relations. Freshly, the English translation of this book has been published by Oxford University Press. So, it is only our critic's ignorance to declare Vikram Seth or Neel Mukherjee as premier writers of gay sexuality in literature. These are only two illustrations.

Bringing It All Together...

The research does not aim to prove the superiority or inferiority of either English writings or regional writings. Rather, it targets to digest English writing into the conventional of Indian writing with a status of Indian individuality. 'Indianness' should be a theme built only for identifying Indian writings. So for R.K. Narayan's time, Indian Writing in English could never be considered foreign from

Indian writings. Neither Tagore nor Amrita Pritam was treated as vernacular authors. Kamla Das effectively managed to write both in English and Malayalam. Nobody asked what language a writer was writing; whether he was Krishna Chandra or Sadat Hassan Monto. They were writing in Urdu but their writings were reachable easily in Hindi and English as well. Indian Writing in English at that time was not named with lingua franca but with the characteristics of Indianness. But newly, Indian writings in other languages, which are available in English, are held off, keeping in mind that they are not in black and white in English.

English enjoys the status of the relating language to the superficial world and also is a necessary instrumental media to converse. Presently and after globalization, it has remarkably placed its consequence and never anyone today could define its permanent status as colonial or outsider. While speaking about Indian writings, how can anyone marginalized the writings of Fakir Mohan Senapati, Premchand, Amrita Pritam, T. Shivshankar Pillai, N.T Vasudevan Nair, or Mahashweta Devi when their writings are all available in English? However, an additional view exists in the mind of some intellectuals that the English language isolates a text from its culture of origin. Once, the Indian writer Shashi Deshpande expressed her ideas that the English language is in some ways harmful to Indian culture not because it is the language of the ex-colonizers, but because it has become the language of the advantaged, elite classes in India. She admits that when she writes in English she is aware that her work will reach out to not more than a few English-speaking readers, most of whom will be thinking the way she does. The problem is that if a novelist writes in English with the purpose of changing social background, the language prohibited the poor and down-trodden whose involvement is most desired, and English has no place in the day by day lives of those people.

Another problem is the fact that writing in English also means using a language in which most, or at least many, of its characters do not speak. Though, for many Indian writers, English is no more than the medium through which they convey themselves and through which they can reach a global audience. But it is worth noting that English is the only source where a linkage can be made with global literary fields; even if in India, the readability of literature in English shows a tiny acceptance in spite of the speedy growth of literacy in English and in incomes of urban Indians. So, it should be a wise decision to term Indian Writing in English not as Indian English Literature, but as its original form of Indian Writings available in English.

REFERENCES

1. Iyengar,Srinivasa. *Indian Writing in English.* New Delhi: Sterling Publishers Pvt. Ltd., 1995: P.33. Print.
2. Ibid., p. 103. Print.
3. Naik,M.K. *A History of Indian English Literature.* New Delhi: Sahitya Akademi, 1995: P.52. Print.
4. ibdi p.69. Print.
5. Ibid., p. 129. Print.
6. Iyengar, Srinivasa. *Indian Writing in English.* New Delhi: Sterling Publishers Pvt. Ltd., 1995: P.327. Print.
7. Steiner George. *The Death of Tragedy, Faber and Faber*. London: MacMillan, 1963: p 53. Print.
8. Devy Ganesh. *After Amnesia (in the GN Devy Reader).* Delhi: Orient Blackswan, 2009: p 45. Print.
9. Ibid., p. 52-59. Print.
10. Devy Ganesh. *The Being of Bhasha (in The GN Devy Reader).* Delhi: Orient Blackswan, 2009: p. 11. Print.
11. Ibid., p. 10. Print.
12. Lane Harlan. *The Wild Boy of Aveyron*. London: Granada Publishing, 1979: p 120 Print.
13. Devy Ganesh. *The Being of Bhasha*. Delhi: Orient Blackswan, 2009: p. 3. Print.
14. Ramanujan A.K. *Is There an Indian Way of Thinking? Contributions to Indian Sociology.* New Delhi : Macmillian, 1989: p 41-58. Print.
15. Devy Ganesh. *The Being of Bhasha*. Delhi: Orient Blackswan, 2009: p. 2. Print.

16. Ibid.p 2. Print.

17. Devy Ganesh. *Of Many Heroes (in the GN Devy Reader).* Delhi: Orient Blackswan, 2009: p 20. Print.

18. Linenthal Edward. *Preserving Memory.* New York: Viking Penguin, 1995: p 33. Print.

19. Devy Ganesh. *The Being of Bhasha.* Delhi: Orient Blackswan, 2009: p 14. Print.

20. Stephen Knight. *Form and Ideology in Crime Fiction.* London: MacMillan, 1980; p 78. Print.

21. http:*//www.sierraclub.org/education/leconte/wood*_hr2715_11-15-03.asp

22. *"Natural Visions -Nature on the Coffee Table".* http://www.press.uchicago.edu/Misc/Chicago/173259.html. Accessed on 15/11/2015.

23. Montaigne. *Essays Upon Some Verses of Virgil.* New Delhi: Routledge, 1580; p122 Print.

24. Bennett, Tony. ed. *Popular Fiction: Technology, Ideology, Production, Reading.* New York and London: Routledge, 1990: P 9. Print.

25. Radway, Janice. *Reading the Romance: Women, Patriarchy, and Popular Literature.* Chappel Hill: University of North Corolina, 1994: p 9. Print.

External links

Statistics

"Census of India 2001: Data on religion". Government of India (Office of the Registrar General). *http://www.censusindia.gov.in/.* Retrieved 2007-05-28.

"Constitution of India". Government of India (Ministry of Law and Justice). *http://indiacode.nic.in/coiweb/welcome.html. Retrieved 2007-05-28.*

Reports

"International Religious Freedom Report 2006: India".

United States Department of State. *http://www.state.gov/g/drl/rls/irf/2006/71440.htm.* Retrieved 2007-05-28.